One Man and his Band

One Man and his Band

ALAN BARBER

© Alan Barber, 2018

Published by Alan Barber

A CIP catalogue record for this book is available from the British Library.

ISBN 978-1-9996553-0-3

Book layout and cover design by Clare Brayshaw

Prepared and printed by:

York Publishing Services Ltd
64 Hallfield Road
Layerthorpe
York YO31 7ZQ

Tel: 01904 431213

Website: www.yps-publishing.co.uk

CONTENTS

PART ONE

INTRODUCTION

Where does one start on such a task (to write a book covering 50 years), so taking a hint from Julie Andrews in the 'Sound of Music, we'll 'Start at the very beginning', and to coin a phrase from the 'man' himself 'Don't start, join in', we will begin.

Before we do however, and because it is my name on the front cover of this book, I feel it is not only necessary, but my obligation, to explain that without the help of members of the band, both 'old' members and those still existing, and some of those people who have been associated with it, it simply would not have happened.

Therefore, my thanks go to, Delwyn Gane, Andy Pratt, Rosalyn Cox and Emily, Anne Raine, Glyn Griffiths, Robert Needham, Martin Smith, Arthur Lowcock, Catherine Watson, Ken and Glynis Trinder, plus many others, but particularly so for attending the 'get-togethers' to reminisce and help create the story that we are about to read.

My thanks to my sister Joan Barker for help with earlier editions, proof reading and grammatical corrections!

My thanks also go to Mr. Fred Paling, and Mr. Frank Pratt for their contributions, and of course the valuable input provided by Haydn himself.

And, an acknowledgement for a past member Gillian Robinson who created a scrap book which provided an invaluable source of information for those early years of the band.

Finally, as a point of clarification and identity, you will come across various titles for the 'Man in Charge', referred to throughout this book, 'The Boss', 'Griff', Haydn or simply 'HG', but all relate to the same person – Mr. Haydn Griffiths MBE, Conductor of Armthorpe Elmfield Band.

I hope that you find the history of Armthorpe Elmfield Band both interesting and entertaining.

Please join me.

CHAPTER I

OVERTURE – THE JOURNEY COMMENCES

Haydn's great passion in life is music, and as you will soon learn, there was an element of tradition in the Griffiths' household. Haydn's father Edwin (Senior) was a trombone player and conductor of the local Colliery Band – Markham Main, and Haydn's brothers, Edwin who was secretary of the band at the time we are talking about played solo trombone and Horace another brother played bass trombone.

Haydn Griffiths 1946

It was of no surprise therefore that Haydn followed the family banding tradition but rather than play trombone he played cornet. He started his playing career at the age of 6 and was a member of Markham Main Colliery Band by the age of 7. His first engagement was for King George IV's Silver Jubilee in May 1935. Haydn was appointed principle cornet for the band at the age of 14 which he held for 19 years and became conductor at 29. During these formative years he was in great demand both as a guest player and soloist in and around South Yorkshire. It must be said that because of his versatility as a player, it enabled him to play in most local dance bands and orchestras of the time, including on one occasion playing solo trumpet in Handel's Messiah. Haydn's first 'live' broadcast I am told was with Grimethorpe Colliery Band at the age of 17, and he recalls only having a balance test for a rehearsal. Other bands requesting his assistance were Carlton Main, Cresswell, Grimethorpe, Thorne, Rossington and Yorkshire Main Colliery to name but a few.

Markham Main Colliery Band 1940

The Griffiths, Haydn, Edwin (Senior), Edwin, Horace

Similarly, some of the dance bands of that era that Haydn played with include, Blue Quavers, High Hatters, Mervyn Milton, Maurice Potter, Grand Embassy and Alex Berry. Again, only a selection!

Markham Main Quartet: Haydn Griffiths, Sid Potter, Edwin Griffiths (senior), Edwin Griffiths, Horace Griffiths.

Edwin (Senior), Haydn's father took Markham Main Band from the 'fourth section' into Championship Class during his leadership of the band. This family tradition was to continue when at the age of 19 Haydn was appointed Assistant Band Master of Markham Main Colliery Band.

Haydn became bandmaster of Hatfield Colliery Band (another local band) when he was 27, but continued to play for Markham Main and became their band master at the age

Haydn Griffiths 1947

of 29. He remained a member of this Armthorpe Colliery Band for 32 years and guided them (following in his father's footsteps) to many National Championships during the late 50's and early 60's.

Back Row: Don Parker, Les?, Johnny Harrison, Front Row: Haydn, Frank ?, Bill Snowden.

It is now over 50 years ago since this story started, and as said, Haydn Griffiths was conductor of Markham Main Colliery Band. At that time, they were giving some of the popular well-known bands such as Grimethorpe, Brodsworth, Brighouse & Rastrick a run for their money.

It was during this period then in the early 60's that Mr. Griffiths used to attend the local school on a couple of afternoons each week teaching school children how to play a brass instrument, and it was also around that time that my best friend John Middleton who happened to be the Godson of Haydn Griffiths and already in the band convinced me to join too.

Trying to work out a time line back from when I left school in 1968 I guess that I would be in the Junior School which does coincide with vague recollections of when I was in Mrs Keithley's class being the first year of the Junior Boys School around 1959-60. She 'quizzed' me on one occasion when I had asked permission to go to the band practice, as to what instrument I played. "Baritone, Miss" was my reply. She said, "that's not an instrument it's a singer!!"

Armthorpe School Band 1959

Delia Plummer, Sylvia Turgoose

The junior Band in the 1980s

Every Tuesday and Thursday all would be 'budding' brass bandsmen would go to one of the school halls to practice on some very old instruments. My first memories of this very early time is that as you progressed as a learner in the local school band practices, you would be invited to the band hut in the colliery grounds on a Saturday afternoon where you would literally 'paste' music onto card and then sit and listen to the big band, Markham Main, practice with the assumption that if you got good enough then that is where you would finish up.

This was to change because in 1964 Haydn decided to follow his heart and concentrate on forming a band from this younger generation of band enthusiasts.

The band hut at the colliery had very good acoustics, whether this had been introduced when building I guess we will never know, but I can remember on occasions practicing there when we started to play in competitions, and I can now mention that it is being used today for practices 50 years later for reasons I will explain later.

First public appearance of Armthorpe High School Band by permission of the headmaster Mr. Winterton, was at a coffee evening at the Gertrude Bell Hall last Tuesday. Members, aged nine to 15, are, solo cornets, G. Griffiths, G. Thompson, C. Downing; second cornets, R. Needham, N. Downing; third cornets, P. Paling, G. Davison; horns, D. Gane, M. Styles, B. Dinning; euphoniums, T. Elison, J. Middleton, A. Barber; bass, A. Lowcock, I. Boughey; percussion, Miss S. Fletcher. More than £20 was raised for the Church Ladies Sewing Guild.

Cutting of unknown date recording first public performance

Initially the Band was known as Armthorpe School band, made up mainly of pupils from the secondary school and of course Glyn Griffiths (Haydn's son). Glyn used to join us even from the infant school, and is still a member today thereby continuing the Griffiths family tradition.

Over the next couple of years as well as practicing at Armthorpe School, Haydn was asked to continue his peripatetic activities at a youth club in Doncaster and invited to teach music at Elmfield House Youth Club, so he had in effect two junior bands. This continued for a while, and the following is an extract that I have found from a newspaper cutting dating back to the time in question.

THE Elmfield House Youth Club brass band.

They have no uniforms and are always short of instruments, but the brass band composed of youngsters from Armthorpe Schools and Elmfield House Youth Club blow as enthusiastically as any that ever won a national championship. And wherever they go they are loudly applauded in this mining district where brass bands are part of tradition.

Conducting them gives great satisfaction to Mr. Haydn Griffiths, visiting teacher of brass instruments at Armthorpe High School, and once bandmaster of the prizewinning Markham Main Colliery Band.

'I enjoy teaching children', he says. 'Like me, they are adventurous in the tunes they want to play. One of their favourites is Edelweiss. Brass Bands should be more versatile, suiting the audience, but when you try this in some adult bands, the 'old guard' are against you.

That was very much the case for a long time whilst brass bands were often very popular, quite often the music they played as 'typical' band music sometimes in my opinion can be quite 'heavy'.

Principal cornet in the youth band is another of the musical Griffiths, whose ancestors came from Wales – Haydn's 11-year-old son, Glyn. Glyn likes to play the tunes from 'The Sound of Music' so this gives you an indication of the time we are talking about! (The Sound of Music was arranged by Rogers and Hammerstein and made into a film which was released on 29th March 1965).

Arranging music based on the popular tunes of the day became the 'thing' for Haydn as you will learn later.

CHAPTER 2

IN THE EARLY DAYS

In the early days, and at the time it was stated that there were 22 young musicians, aged from 9 to 15, plus 11 beginners, and continuing from the article,

those who cannot attend the school sessions go to Elmfield House, where they are often joined by pupils from other schools.

A quote from another article relating back to this period stated,

On Monday, the Youth Band played for the pleasure of Kirk Sandall's old folk and will soon entertain those of Armthorpe. They have recently taken part in a school concert and played at a coffee morning for Armthorpe Parish Council and Garden parties are on their agenda.

This I guess reflects the start or the beginnings.

It was typical of the band's audiences' and of engagements in the early years… around 1966 and all that. I suppose that I should explain. You probably realize that the National sport of Great Britain is football but unfortunately, we do not seem to do very well these days. Anyway, back in the days of the Armthorpe Elmfield Band (AEB) in and around the 70's we had a very strong football atmosphere in the band. Conversations at band practice night would revolve around the football that had been played at the weekend, and of course many of the band were keen supporters of the sport. We can even boast that we had a player at one of our band gatherings, who was the Captain of Liverpool and went on to captain England. (See story about the 'Hot Dog' Supper).

Anyway, I cannot leave this section without at least mentioning some of the keen and avid supporters of the leading clubs of that time. Whilst it bears no significance to the progress and success of the band, it did have a bearing (sometimes) on how well the band played!

Glyn Griffiths – Manchester City, Eddie Mangham – Tottenham Hotspurs, Mick Harding – West Ham, John Middleton – Leeds United, Steve Robinson – Manchester City.

Concert performance from 1969

It was not unknown for some of the band to wear their supporter's scarves during practice especially if two of the teams had been playing each other at the weekend. In fact, there was so much rivalry at times concerning Manchester City, Tottenham and West Ham, I think the 'Boss' wrote a piece of music following a particular game – Something to do with 'Blowing Bubbles'!

Anyway, carrying on, it should be noted that for a while the bands did operate separately and it wasn't until about 1975 that it actually became one. Competitions that were entered in the early days were under the name of either Armthorpe Band or Elmfield House Youth Band as can be seen in some of the programmes of the time. The article below is taken from a newspaper cutting dating to this period which provides evidence that the band did in fact operate until at least 1973 as two separate bands (even though the same people played in both Bands).

Newspaper cutting, dated May 1973. The article was written by Jim Robinson, who for many years was Deputy Leader at Elmfield House Youth Club.

The brass band of a Doncaster Youth Club has had spectacular success by winning two music festivals in the same day. Two hours and a quick trip down the A1 separated Elmfield House Youth Clubs double victory in brass sections of Pontefract and Worksop music festivals.

For the 31 members of the band, average age 14, the hectic evenings playing was the result of a change of date for the Pontefract festival. 'We had entered both and thought we would have to drop out of one, but Pontefract agreed to have the brass band section earlier to give us time to get to Worksop' said deputy leader Jim Robinson.

Their playing conducted by Haydn Griffiths was greeted with enthusiasm by adjudicators at both festivals. At Pontefract, the band played Handel's Royal Fireworks Music and at Worksop Dennis Wright's Mozart style Salzburg Suite".

During these early days, we continued to practice at school but also on certain nights each week would take the bus to Doncaster and attend the Youth Club for further practice. It did of course open the band to additional members who did not attend the local Comprehensive School at Armthorpe. The band grew in numbers getting people from other surrounding schools, Danum Grammar, Doncaster Grammar, Wheatley Hills and as time went on many other schools and associations from the area.

Arthur Lowcock now a past player but member of the band for many years recalls that "When we were youngsters and travelling to Elmfield House in Doncaster we would have to go on the bus, but we did get a lift home in parents' cars". Arthur says that he remembered on one occasion that there were ten kids in Haydn's car, a Vauxhall Viva – JDT 729 (which stands for John Don't Trump, 7 plus 2 = 9 and the reason we can remember the registration so well). Del was laid on top of a bass and Glyn was in the boot. I must confess that this is a slight exaggeration because at a recent gathering of some of the older members this very incident was discussed and "Arthur it wasn't 10, it was 8," but Robert Needham seems to think, "it was 9." (It was a fair few any way!)

On another occasion, we were reminded that when time came to go home, it was so foggy that you could not see a hand in front of you as they say. On that occasion Ivor Boughey had to walk in front of the car and Arthur had to walk at the side telling the driver (Griff) where to go.

However, in attending Elmfield House and now being part of the Doncaster 'catchment' area, it also increased the geographical area where we would be asked to play. In the early days, it was often at local Church concerts and 'Old' Folks Christmas Parties or a Summer Garden Party here and there, and of course we had to perform at the annual school concerts. However, it started to change and 'Our' performing areas also increased, and became more widespread and varied.

Flaxton, Beehive Buses coach in the background.

In the garden of the 'White House' in Armthorpe.

In the grounds of the former Methodist Chapel in Armthorpe.

1973 Westwoodside

13

In those early days (and probably because we did not have an extensive repertoire to fill the programme) we would have additional acts to give us a 'break', or really to add some variation and 'padding' to the programme. Mr Ivan Stanger would often join us and perform recitals such as *Albert and the Lion*, and on other occasions Ken Trinder a member of the band who joined us from Danum School, would stand up and sing a ballad or two. Ken Trinder picks up the story and explained that he had appeared at a local church fete as a hippy and minstrel, Griff persuaded him to be a fortune teller at the Hot Dog Supper. Glynis (already a band member) then 'dragged' him along to a rehearsal and Griff, knowing of Ken's many talents, decided to put them to good use and managed to convince him to do something similar during our concerts as well as take up the trombone. We also had David Prescott playing the clarinet winning audiences over with the likes of Aker Bilk's – 'Stranger on the Shore'. David eventually finished up marrying Liz Parke (a band member), as you will see later.

I continue with the story, and whilst we mention some of the Bands traditions (particularly at christmas time) a little later, it is worth mentioning here if only to emphasize the qualitative nature inherent in the Griffiths family that on one occasion whilst we were playing outside the house of Mr Griffiths Senior, during our Christmas Eve tour of the Streets of Armthorpe - carolling, Haydn was called across by his father who said, one of your horn player's is out of tune – flat. Haydn in relaying the conversation to us just said, not bad for an 84-year old, is it?

The Band was growing as indeed was its reputation, so it was time to start formalising the band structure with a Secretary Eddie Mangham (Senior), Alan Humphries, Band Treasurer and a supporting team from several other parents. Frank Pratt, Chairman, who later became Music Announcer, a role he would undertake for many years, and the President of the Band, a local Armthorpe Councillor, Mr Harry Schofield. Support came in other ways, from Fred and Barbara Paling, the use of their house and extensive garden for a Griff idea (the Hot Dog Supper) see reference later –'the seasons of the band', Sid and June Smith, Derek Boyes, father of Richard, Steve and Chris. With this came various support from places of work, like the Coal Board, Yorkshire Electricity Board (Barnby Dun power station) International

Harvesters, Bingham's, British Rail, where things were begged, borrowed or purloined but perhaps we should not say any more about that!!

Frank Pratt has his own memories of the band and his association with it. He writes;

'My first experience of Armthorpe High School band as it was originally called was soon after my appointment as the Clerk of Armthorpe Parish Council in 1966. Christmas was marked by the council tea and a concert for the older people of the Village and entertainment was by the band led by Haydn Griffiths.

Frank goes on to say;

I thought the band was brilliant as did the pensioners. Not too long afterwards our younger son Neil, came home enthused for membership of the band to be followed soon after by his brother Andrew who in 2015 completed 45 years continuous playing. I (Frank) was drawn into supporting Neil and Andrew, taking them and friends to and from Elmfield House Youth Club for rehearsals. Concerts were either played under the name of Armthorpe High School Band or Elmfield House Band. The players were the same and Haydn also taught at Elmfield House.

In 1974 /75 the Elmfield House Band represented Doncaster in a competition for the title of 'Boys Club of the Year'. Sadly, we could only play the lads and not the girls Frank explains, but they (the Girls) came along and enjoyed the contest at the Royal Festival Hall. The band played "Rejoicings" from the Royal Fireworks suite followed by "Power to all our Friends" and finally "Match of the Day" and we were declared winners. Doncaster also took second place when Martin Hughes sang brilliantly. His path (Martin Hughes) to fame saw him turn professional both in Britain and later in the USA. (We refer to this competition later in the book.)

He continues by saying, 'that was a Monday night to remember' and the band returned home on the Tuesday and played a concert for pensioners in Woodlands another local mining village near to Doncaster. Two days off school led to criticism from the head of the

School and sanctions against the band, so it was decided to go it alone without the support of the School. (Another reason for our departure/ separation from the school was the fact that some of the older members who had left school had started to grow their hair as was fashionable at the time and Mr Stephenson the head of the school was very much against young people with long hair) We soon sorted out a new name as he says – the "Armthorpe Elmfield Band". Doncaster Youth Service which came from our association with Elmfield House Youth Club continued its support and help, in particular people such as Tony Socket, Ron Bailey, Jim Robinson and their Staff.

From the start Haydn had persuaded one of his neighbours to volunteer to be Secretary – Eddie Mangham. Eddie Mangham was enthusiastic, capable and earned the affection of the players. Frank continues and says, "I am not sure how I became Chairman, but I did and served a long number of years including writing the constitution of the Band Parents Association, and then acted as Treasurer to follow Alan Humphries."

Finally, Frank's recollections point out that

> "It was all made pleasurable by the bands musical achievements, and the financial efforts to protect the bands independence despite encountering many difficulties. Music in schools needs to be nurtured for the good and well- being of youngsters either as soloists or members of bands, orchestras and groups. AEB has demonstrated its value to the community and long may it continue."

CHAPTER 3

STRUGGLES OF THE BAND –
INSTRUMENTS TAKEN BACK

Further evidence of the struggles of the band's earlier years can be seen in this letter from Mr Mangham the Secretary to the Parents inviting them to become Patrons.

Dear,

In 1964 Mr Haydn Griffiths decided to give the opportunity for young people to form their own Brass Band and so was formed the Armthorpe High School Band. Many of the young people were also members of the Elmfield House Youth Club and also played for the Elmfield Youth Band again under the leadership of Mr Griffiths.

In 1974 and again in 1975 difficulties arose over the use of instruments belonging either to another Band or to the High School and it was therefore decided that the parents of Band members and many supporters, would accept responsibility for raising the money necessary to buy replacement instruments. The target was achieved, and it was then decided to re-name the Band as The Armthorpe Elmfield Band. Under this name the Band has gone from success to success and in 1975 the competition results were as follows:

1ˢᵗ place   Yorkshire 4ᵗʰ Section, Mineworker's Contest.

1ˢᵗ place   4ᵗʰ Section National Mineworker's Championships.

Radio Sheffield 'Bold as Brass' Contest- best 4th Section Band and Trophy winners

Gold Award Northern National Association of Boys Clubs

A recent development has been the formation of an Association whose objectives are to help the Band by providing instruments, uniforms and generally meet the considerable expenses involved. The property bought in the past by the parents and supporters is now held in the names of the Trustees of the Association. Over £1200 was spent in 1975 on Instruments and in 1976 we need over £1400 to replace four old instruments.

In addition to the contest successes the Band has given over 60 concerts in 1975. Certain of these were prestige engagements at places like Harrogate, Skegness, Knaresborough, Morecambe and Liverpool as well as in the Doncaster area but the majority were on a voluntary basis for local organisations. This will continue to be the practice even though the band has improved its status in the brass band ratings.

Not only do the band members receive first class musical training they are also able to travel around the country and whilst this might embarrass them they have proved to be first class ambassadors for the Armthorpe area and continually receive much praise not only for their musical ability but for the way in which they conduct themselves. Musical training goes hand in hand with character development and this point is recognized by many people who wish their children to join the band.

Our Association is now seeking to enrol Patrons and it has been suggested that you might be interested in being one of our Patrons. The subscription fee has been kept quite low at £1 per annum minimum. We do very much hope that we might look forward to your support and you will consent to become a Patron.

It is our intention to keep all the Patrons informed about forthcoming events and achievements.

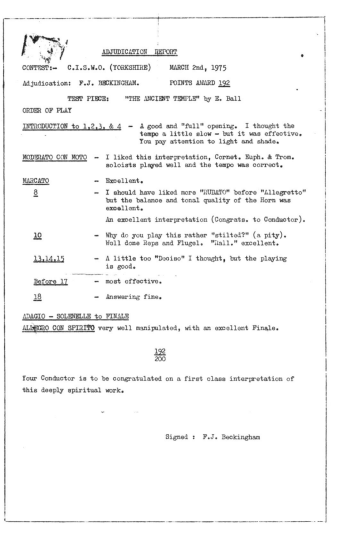

Adjudicators comments

This article then provided testimony that as long ago as 1975 the Band did a considerable amount of travelling, entertaining many and usually on a voluntary basis.

On the 5th December of that year another letter came out following a general meeting of parents and it was decided to form the Band Parents Association and to adopt a proper constitution. The letter stated

"Most of you will have had a copy of the draft constitution but if not and you want one then please let me know."

(See appendix 1)

The Constitution and rules were written by Frank way back in 1974/75 and were revised and formally approved again by the Association at a meeting held on 19th Day of April 1994, and were updated at a meeting held on 25th Day of September 2007.

The original trustees we believe were Nigel Stevenson head master at the Comprehensive School and Ron Bailey, head of Elmfield House and part of Doncaster Youth Service.

The success of the Band is that not only does it do well musically, but we have over the years shown clearly that the parents and supporters are willing to work hard to meet the need for instruments, uniforms, transport etc.

The letter went on,

Most of you know that we had to go into debt to buy replacement instruments for the Band, but thanks to all the hard work we have now paid for those instruments and remember the cost was about £1200. Whilst the Band continues to have the practical support of Elmfield House in so many ways it was realized in 1973 that no longer could the band exist based on using instruments belonging to Schools and other Bands. Experience has showed that a change of policy could leave the band without instruments and this is not acceptable.

It was important to make some arrangements to safeguard ownership of instruments and other property bought with money raised by or for the band. This was another important purpose of the constitution.

It is recognized that all of us derive a great deal of pleasure and satisfaction from our involvement with the band and whilst this work is heavy at times the interest is always there and our way of working together must be second to none.

We are not out of the wood yet'. The members of the band continue to grow not only in numbers but in size! The band needs more blazers, and also some replacement instruments as they move up into the Third Section for the 1976 Contest.

One final article from a newspaper cutting of this time states:

'Parents dig deep to keep school band at the top', and relates to the band having to return some instruments that had been loaned to them years before.

Parents have come to the rescue of a prize winning junior band at Armthorpe, who were crippled when nine of their top instruments were reclaimed by the original owners, the Markham Main Colliery Band.

They have already pooled together £200 to buy new instruments in time for the start of band practices in the autumn term, but are still in need of £700 to pay the bill in full.

The school Band started to use instruments provided by the Markham Main Brass Band several years ago when youngsters were first encouraged to play by the late Mr Edwin Griffiths, father of the school band's present conductor, who was also the Markham conductor.

The instruments have remained with the school players since but in recent months discussions between the school and the colliery have led to the original nine being taken back.

Now the parents have come to the rescue, there is no danger of a sudden collapse of the band occurring in the same way again. Mr Tom Gibson, general manager of Markham Main Colliery and chairman of their general welfare committee, told the Gazette that the instruments used by the school were originally bought through the Coal Industry Social Welfare Organisation scheme.

'The last thing we wanted to do was to stop the youngsters having the facilities to play in the band', he told the newspaper.

Band organisers at the pit would have liked the High School players to have become part of the junior section of the Markham Main Band, but they were never able to tie up the loose ends for this to take place.

Had the school band joined forces with the Markham Brass Band, there could have been more chance of them gaining assistance through the parent welfare scheme of the pit.

Mr Mangham, the High School Band secretary, said that they had never heard anything official about becoming part of the Markham set-up, but the parents committee did feel that the instruments did belong to the Coal Board and that they were entitled to have them back, he added.

Without dwelling on the fact that the instruments were taken back at a time when the band was in its infancy and just starting to become recognized, what further exasperated the issue that there was no warning, it was from immediate effect. To say the band was not for-warned on the day in question is borne out by the fact that Haydn had gone down the pit and when he surfaced he was summoned immediately to a meeting at the Welfare in front of representatives from CISWO, Colliery Management, Council members etc to be told that if the band adopted the name Markham Main Junior Band they could keep the instruments, if not they would be taken back. And this is what happened with immediate effect.

This is probably the first problem that the band had to encounter and as the reader will learn it certainly wasn't the last.

Eddie Mangham (Senior) continued,

'The school band consists of 29 boys and 2 girls, and now fulfils a minimum of 50 engagements each year earning up to £25 for appearances at local galas and shows.'

The band finished runners up in their first band contest three years ago, and have since chalked up wins at the Worksop Festival and the junior section of the Coal Board contest at Sheffield. Their next contest is to be in Blackpool when they will be lining up against bands, including senior bands from many parts of the country.

With support from the parents who are prepared to raise £900 to save the Armthorpe High School Band, and enable them to continue are now fast becoming one of the top junior bands in South Yorkshire, and resulted in not having to curtail their impressive list of annual engagements.

You will continue to hear about the support the band has had over the years from the parents of the band members, and you will hear also of many other occasions when the band has had hardships and difficult times to deal with, as indeed what has happened recently. But with the continual comradeship of those in the band and those still associated with it, Armthorpe Elmfield Band overcomes these problems and as you will hear, continues to provide entertainment far and wide, playing between 60 – 80 engagements a year.

First official Band Photograph in the Grounds of Elmfield House 1975.

CHAPTER 4

TO END THE BEGINNING!

So as we enter the finale to this opening Overture, it has to be said that it would be very difficult to name everyone who has been a member of the band, and any omissions should not be taken as a 'snub', because often the names mentioned are with regard to an 'occurrence' or amusing incident that happened at a particular time or event during the life of the Band, or who, in some cases are still members of the band, 50 years, on, whom I will rely on for information to add to this book.

Names like,

A   Alan Alberry, Brain Alberry, Ray Alberry, Gary Adshead, Mr. Andrews, Paul Adshead, Nigel Alberry, Glyn Andrews

B   Michael Buckley, Colin Butler, Richard Boyes, Steve Boyes, Chris Boyes, Ivor Boughey, Edward Beard, James Beard, Helen Boyes, Trudie Brookes, Mark Bailey, Steven Brocklesby, Claire Beevor (Fairhurst), Dianne Buckley, Jenny Booth, Angie Baker, Sharon Burt, Andrew Baker, Chris Browne, Simon Baker, Bill Best, Alan Barber, Marie Bettes, Alison Buttesworth

C   Steve Cunningham, Maurice Cann, Rosalyn Cox, Hayden Carter, ? Cheetham, Lynn Colbourn, Emily Cox, Jamie Caygill, James Carter,

D Chris Downing, Nick Downing, Denis Draycott, Harald Deville, , Andrea Davison, Ian Dawn, Chris Davis, James Davies, Alan Darley

E Terry Elson who unfortunately is not with us any more

F Sue Fletcher

G Del Gane, Glyn Griffiths, Glynis Giles later to become Trinder, Paul Gofton, Charlie Gibson, Chris Gammons, Catherine Gilbert (Watson) Karen Goften, Tim Gammons, David Griffiths, Ann Louise Griffiths, Jane Gammons, Paul Gorton, Scot Godfrey, Leanne Garland, Helen Gilbert, John Gray, Russ Guest, Pete Guest

H Michael Harding, Neil Humphries, Katherine Holt, Sarah Hickson, Joanne Hole, Glen Helliwell, John Hodgson, Roy Havenhand, Julian Hollings. Fiona Hulbert, Tom Hodby, Paul Hope, Steve Huggins, Andrew Hollings, Graham Hole

J Mathew Jones, Simon Johnson, Steve Jobe, Angela Jenkinson, Paul Jenkinson

K Ray Kilcoyne, Katy Mitchell. Bernard Kelsey, George King, Tom Kennedy, Terry Kilcoyne

L Alan Lowe, Arthur Lowcock, Chris Leader, Mervyn Lloyd

M Eddie Mangham, Julie Mawson, Paul Makinson, John Middleton, Lucy Monks, Kelly Magee, Sarah Maw, Katie Mitchell, Paul Mather, John Monks, Dave Macfaddon, John Monks, Stuart Marley, Lee Moses, Yvonne Marly, Emma Mann

N Robert (Bob) Needham, Eleanor Nagle,

P Andy Pratt, Neil Pratt, Paul Paling, Derek Paling, Sue (Parkes), Steve Prescott, Delia Plummer, Dan Pearson, Simon Pollard, Syd Potter, David Panks, Liz Parke later to become Liz Prescott

Q Chloe Queen

R Steve Robinson, Gillian Robinson to become Barber, Carl Ryan, Ian Robinson, Malcolm Robinson, Adam Rosbottom,

Anne Raine, Sarah Raine, Adrian Rosbottom,
Abigail Rosbottom, Graham Rawson, Anne Marie Rigby,
Simon Robinson, Joanne Rimmington, Mr Rawson, Karl Ryan,
Richard Rawson,

S   Martin Smith, Ann Sargeson, John Surtess, Chris Snowden,
Julie Smith, Helen Snowden, Samantha Stenson

T   Ken Trinder, Jonathon Tingay, Brian Temple, Sylvia Turgoose,
Malcolm Trimmingham, Luke Tyas, Brian Temple,
Daniel Townend, Luke Tyass, Alicia Tissington

W   Graham (Jim) Wildey as he was always known! Adrian Wilson,
Thomas Wigley, Richard Wigley, Shannon Watson,
Ian Wilson, Laura Wilkinson, Lyn Wheeliker, Marcel Webster,
Eamon Wilson, Jack Waterhouse,

the list goes on!

35 28

ARMTHORPE ELMFIELD BAND?
SKEGNESS

PLAYERS STANDING L-R.   SEATED L-R

Steve Boys   Glyn Griffiths
Rij Parke   Steve Prescot
Paul Gofton   Chris Gammon,
. Steve Robinson   . Brian Temple
. John Birtees   . Brian Cann
. Tim Gammon   Chris Boys
. Ian Robinson   Male Robinson
. Alan Dorkey   Rick Boys
Rib. Needham   Mich Buckley
Ian Finley   Len Elcan
H. GRIFFITHS — Gillian Robinson   Martin Smith
Neil Pratt.   Neil Humphries.
Maurice Cann   Graham Wildey
Mich Harding   Del. Gane
Neil Humphries A. Pratt.
Eddie Mangham

Gillians Scrap Book 3
June 1974

PART TWO

PRELUDE

CHAPTER 5

MOVING ON

We are most fortunate with the friends and supporters that we have had, and to say that we were a big happy family in the band is one way of putting it, and the fact that we relied on support from parents and friends cannot be emphasized enough. It is brought home how important this was for Haydn and his band in this next comment from Catherine Watson (nee Gilbert) another past player who has contributed to some of the funny stories that we shall get to later in the book. Catherine says,

> *"My dad reminded me that one year (late 80's around 1987) when he had been made redundant, the band paid for Mum and Dad to come to London with us as we were playing in the National Finals at Hammersmith and it was to be the first time that I was playing a solo part on the Flugel Horn."*

This story is probably one of many times that Mr G acknowledged the support the parents gave of their time and energy helping the band, running band members around etc, (Taxiing is the word used these days!) 'And he made this gesture at a time when he knew my family were under financial pressure.' This is one of many such gestures that Haydn made in thanking his back-room staff and support.

I remember from long ago when Helen Turner (who later became Mrs Boyes) who played principle cornet for many years coming to the band as a youngster with her grandmother on the bus.

You will hear of coincidences and bizarre meetings as we progress through the book and my (AB's) meeting and first contact with Catherine is equally interesting. Catherine took her daughter Amber to a local Montessori nursery where it just so happened my daughter Nicky worked. Nicky looked after Amber and it was during a conversation that the band was mentioned, and it was also mentioned that Nicky did not have a mum, and Catherine a junior member of the band when Nicky's Mum died put 2 and 2 together and realized she knew me. So, moving on to my Granddaughters Birthday Party this bouncing bundle of fun came bounding up saying I know you, you used to be in Armthorpe Elmfield Band. The rest is history as they say. Thank you for that Catherine and thank you for the many stories and memories you have shared with us.

You will hear more about the support I am sure as we progress through the years, and as Frank Pratt alluded to earlier that the band became and is still a 'self-financing' band thereby relying on this support, generosity and general fund raising. That said, the band has performed at thousands of concerts over the years raising money for charity and other charitable organisations. (The average number of appearances in a year is usually between 60-80)

So, as we move on during this developing period we started working towards a 'Uniform' for the Band. Previously we had worn grey trousers / skirts and white shirts which were generally the School Uniform. I can't remember the tie that we adopted first, but eventually we progressed to a blazer. When Armthorpe Elmfield Band started wearing blue blazers, this was quite definitely getting 'out of the box' and going against traditions that were usually seen in the banding world. Again, this was another example of Haydn Griffiths showing that he was not 'adverse' to change, or doing something different. When we got the blazers, we did go for grey trousers / skirt and red shirts with round collars and wide white ties! You may see evidence of this on some of the photographs shown in the book. Not long after getting the new uniform we started to really push the boat out and go

32

'up-market' because we also decided to have our own banner to drape over our music stand which proudly stated Armthorpe Elmfield Band. Colin Wilson who was a successful local builder and parent of one of our band members, Adrian, together with his good lady Marjory assisted in providing these. This was obviously after the combination of the two Bands so must have been around 1975/1976.

CHAPTER 6

THE BAND – AN INSTITUTION

The band became not just a band, but an institution with a family atmosphere, and whilst it would be fair to say that it perhaps does not have quite the same intimacy today there is absolutely no question about the loyalty that still remains amongst the band members, old band members, supporters, and local village folk.

Haydn always gave 150 percent and still does, but, he also expected the same commitment from his band and therefore there was no such thing as privacy, and as mentioned in other parts of the book, sometimes disagreements occurred because when some members started to have 'lives' outside the band this did not always suit. An example of the 'closeness' of those earlier days in the band is given here and relates to a little story concerning myself whilst in the bath, and as said with Griff it was all or nothing and there was certainly no such thing as, you will have to wait I am having a bath. I remember one day getting home from work and jumping into the bath. (I don't think showers had really been invented in houses then and most certainly not the double showers that you get today so he couldn't have got in the shower even if they had). I seemed to recall that we had something on that night, anyway here I am in the bath doing the things that one does in the bath and in comes Griff into our house, 'where is he Rene?' (my mother's name), having a bath is the answer. Bathrooms were also downstairs where we lived, so in he walks, 'we have a concert at such and such a time, get ready and can you pick up so and so. Meet at 18.30. This was never regarded as an intrusion; it was just the way it was, and it's fair to say, if someone had a problem, generally everyone had one too, but obviously this was more appropriate for the senior members and/or supporters. The same can be seen throughout, as you have heard from Catherine above of her father's particular problem when the Band was playing in London.

Catherine also reminded me of a story which happened to her when she had a visitor, her Uncle Haydn! Catherine, another Railway worker, worked in Gresley House which used to be adjacent to Doncaster Railway Station and once had a visit from her Uncle Haydn. Well actually Catherine doesn't have an Uncle Haydn (or not one she was aware of) but Griff wanted to show her a new garment cover which had the AEB Logo on, so he reported to Gresley House and Catherine had a call from reception advising her that her Uncle Haydn was in reception and would like to see her.

Delwyn had a similar experience not long before he retired when he was entertaining some foreign customers at his place of work. During a factory visit there was an announcement that a Mr Haydn Griffiths was waiting for him at reception. On hearing this someone in the factory said, you must play for Armthorpe Elmfield Band!

So, from then to more recent times like now, the band, after 25 years of having an ideal base for a band room – in the centre of Armthorpe (where it all began) were faced with an eviction order. Please be assured that it is by no means any wrong doing by the band, but purely the 'want' of the local Headmaster who wished to take back the use of the building. Consequently, we were left with quite a problem because as well as the 3500 musical arrangements, there are spare uniforms, spare instruments, a trailer for transporting all the equipment, tubular bells and a big bass drum, plus everything else one might find in a very active brass band. Not only is the band being evicted it had less than 1 month to do it. But as this was written 25 days after receiving the notification, in Robert Needham's words (mentioned later) – we sorted that, job done. With a lot of hard work and managerial input from the 'Gaffer' who had just escaped from hospital following an operation, we succeeded in getting everything out and re-located, albeit temporary in some cases, for example in 'Ones' Garages, but we have carried out what has been asked, and currently working on the future? Interestingly enough, whilst researching information for this book, I have found a letter from Eddie Mangham who as I said was the secretary at the beginning, and to quote from his letter dated 6th September 1976,

To all Band members,

The next practice will be held in the F.E. Block – Mere Lane on Friday 10th at 7.15pm. (this was where the band room was located for the last 25 years)

It is requested that you attend to: –

Sign the Blackpool contest form

Prepare the programme for the Saturday engagement at the Racecourse.

The Saturday's event will be a special one to celebrate the 200th running of the St Leger.

The Royal Marine Band will also be in attendance, they will give a display parade at 12-30 – 1.00, and 'Beat Retreat' at 5.00pm.

Regarding the band room situation, I will now provide an up-date, several months later because the problem will not be resolved before the book is finished. From the initial eviction from the accommodation that the band had occupied for the last 25 years, the temporary storage facility for some of the spare instruments, and promise of the use of the local Community Centre for rehearsals things have not gone quite according to plan. The use of the Community Centre for Friday night practice did not quite work out because at the time this was to commence the room had been 'let out' for some occasion or other. This happened several times, so it was decided to have the Friday night practice where they had the Wednesday night practice in a spare room in the Wheatsheaf Public House. This again shows the support from local business and thanks must go to Donna and Colin who run the pub for their generosity. But again, this was with restrictions because access was up an emergency staircase on the outside of the building which is not ideal when carrying a 'double b', Bass drum or having an 80odd year old conductor!

So, we move on, and from early thoughts of what do we do now, the band is actively working to again have a band room of its own, but this time build it. Haydn Griffiths and some of the more senior members are trying to locate land in Armthorpe that would enable this to happen, but again I get the feeling that certain councillors in the community are not necessarily behind the band, for whatever reason and certainly not rushing to the cause. As an example, an ideal piece of land was found not 50 metres from the school that they had just vacated adjacent to the village swimming pool. The triangular piece of land had stood vacant for probably as long as the swimming pool had been there, which I guess must be over 30 years because I remember taking my daughter when she was only a small child and she is now thirty-four. Anyway, after months of waiting, we are now advised that we cannot have it because it may be wanted for a car park sometime in the future! This may be factually correct, but one wonders!!

The band now finds itself in a 'catch 22' situation in that it has some plans and ideas, albeit in their infancy, a builder willing to support us, as indeed an electrical engineer, plumber and plasterer, but it still cannot get approval to use some of the vacant land in Armthorpe that is Council owned. Without the land it is pointless for us to have the plans 'drawn-up' and engage with these people, but as we report this 'things' hopefully may be changing and following a concert where the Civic Mayor of Doncaster, Roz Jones was present and hearing about the bands problems particularly with the slow progress with local Armthorpe councillors has categorically stated that she is totally in support of what we are trying to do and will do what she can to progress the project and start things moving, and only in these last few weeks we have identified a piece of land close to the local Armthorpe Rovers football pitch and facilities. Also, following another forced move (albeit short term due to the Wheatsheaf public house being decorated) the band found themselves practicing in what is now known as the Official's Club which was in the grounds of what was Markham Main Colliery. The Official's Club was borne out of what was once the Ambulance Hall and where Markham Main Band used to practice many years ago. Anyway, Mr Griffiths visited the Club some weeks ago to confirm that it was OK for them to practice again that coming Wednesday and Friday. He was asked how things were going with the band, to which Haydn replied that the band was still without a band room and was waiting to hear from the Council (again) if their latest request had been approved. To that the Club Manager responded with, "What about a piece of the land belonging to the Official's Club?" Following a brief discussion with the committee, who all agreed, it would now appear that we may have two 'irons' in the fire so to speak.

So, as we moved closer to Christmas 2015, 51 years after the start of the band, and having endured many setbacks during that time, assuming that we get the right answers, the band will start work on its own band room so that it may continue providing the entertainment that it has done so for the last half century. And now in 2016 it can be officially recorded that we have a drawing, an architect waiting to draw up the plans, an estimate, and plenty of support from the Trustees and Officials of the 'Officials Club' who will discuss the proposals at their forthcoming Annual General Meeting and report back.

So, after a long 12 months the plans for a Band Room for the band have been finalized, submitted for 'Approval' and awaiting acceptance by Doncaster Council Planning Department. The Band Room will be built adjacent to the 'Officials Club' which was Markham Main Ambulance hall and where Markham Main Colliery Band once held rehearsals.

Thanks go to Paul Billings – Reshape Architects
for his help with all this.

Before leaving this topic, it must be mentioned that from informal 'chatting' to some of the bands previous audiences such as Tickhill Round Table etc. they are willing to support the band and provide a financial donation as soon as the project starts progressing. I can also report that it is the intention to have a fund-raising concert in the Cast Theatre in Doncaster by the famous Black Dyke Band and I am reliably informed that we will not have to pay for the services. Following a recent meeting with Dr Nick Childs the conductor of the

Black Dyke Band, he categorically stated that it is their intention to perform a concert here in Doncaster at the earliest opportunity. The meeting was a great success as well as having the opportunity to listen to them making a recording. To me it reiterated the admiration that Haydn Griffiths has with this world re-known band leader, and fellow bandsmen, as he was treated with the greatest respect from someone who is at the absolute top of the tree in the banding world.

Returning now to the aspirations of 'our' (AE) band it is also the intention to apply for a lottery grant but, as can be appreciated, without the former (acquisition of land) we cannot pursue the latter (build a band hut) but as you will read below, the band has been down this path before when they applied for a grant in-order to provide a greater service to young people in the local community.

The following articles then relate to this and suffice to say the band was very fortunate to be given a lottery grant in 1996 for £53,779.00 for new instruments. I am told that in return the Band had to have a special piece of music arranged, so the St Leger was created which is obviously a fitting name. The total cost of the project was £61,784.00 of which the band contributed £13,383.00. This included an amount of £850.00 spent on the commission of the new music – St Leger.

Newspaper cuttings at the time advised,

'They've got some brass!!'

The Star dated October 21st, 1996 stated that Armthorpe Elmfield Band drummed up some brass – over £50,000 in fact!

"The band has been awarded £53,799 of lottery cash to buy new musical equipment."

The grant from the Arts Council means the band can expand to allow more young musicians a chance to play. A lot of the money is to be spent on expensive percussion items such as timpani drums, vibraphone, tubular bells and a drum kit, as well as covering the costs of a full set of brass instruments, including cornets, trombones and horns.

Chairman of the band (at the time) Phil Hulbert said they had been hopeful of success when they put in the bid a year ago. 'It was nonetheless a very pleasant surprise when we were told we had been successful', he said. 'since we are not sponsored by a company and only receive a small grant from the council, this money is an extremely welcome boost, as it would have taken years to raise ourselves.'

And, if you missed the article on the Monday you could read a similar one on Wednesday 23rd October 1996 (either that or the paper was running short of things to report and needed some more padding!)

Armthorpe Elmfield Band has turned gold into brass, after attracting a huge lottery handout. This meant that the band which had been running for 32 years would be able to take on more young people to improve their talents.

To continue with another little digression and whilst it is not specifically concerning the Band other than the fact that Armthorpe is in Yorkshire – 'Gods Own' Country, and anything associated with Yorkshire is good. I, and I am sure that I say it for the majority of band members that have been associated with the band are proud of that fact. I am a Yorkshireman and proud of it and whilst Griff's family originate from Wales who are indeed a very patriotic nation he has been in Armthorpe since he was six at least so I guess he can be regarded as a Yorkshireman, (I am told however that he was born here so yes he is a Yorkshireman albeit with a slightly Welsh name!) Anyway continuing, having been in some respectable company at times especially when working abroad, I quite often get asked where I am from and because I couldn't really disguise my accent and certainly not the same as William Haigh who is supposed to have a neutral accent can do, I take great pleasure in telling my sometimes-condescending company that the man who climbed that big mountain – 'Mount Everest', well his Grandfather was a Yorkshireman! Oh, and by the way Julie Andrew's singing teacher lived in Leeds. There are obviously many other interesting facts emanating from Yorkshire, none least than winning more medals in the 2012 Olympics than Australia! The fact was reiterated to me at some 'do' or other where it was mentioned that Yorkshire would have been certainly in the top 6 or 8 in the medals table. Oh, and in 2014 we had the start of the Tour du France here in the heart of Yorkshire. Need I say more! We even had royalty joining the thousands that had come to West Tanfield to watch the tour, who then had hamburgers in a local hostelry the Freemasons Arms at Nosterfield.

The point being made is that Armthorpe Elmfield Band have not only represented Doncaster, but Yorkshire in Contests, Competitions and General Entertainment 'preaching' wherever they go the 'Gospel' of the brass band movement. It is fair to say therefore that Haydn Griffiths' reputation goes without saying and as well as the innovative ideas and often different methods that he has introduced, he is particularly keen to maintain the traditions that in today's world often fall by the way side. As an example, marching on St Georges Day, which the Band still do, celebrating Yorkshire Day and more recently the anniversary of the end of the War. For his dedication, he is respected by many associated with the banding world, and you will hear later of some of the best players in the banding world that have given their time to accompany Armthorpe Elmfield Band on stage, but what must be mentioned is that this unprecedented respect is confirmed when he was asked to conduct the world famous Black Dyke Mills Band in Selby Abbey. What an opportunity, and what an occasion.

CHAPTER 7

NEW YEARS HONOURS LIST PAYS TRIBUTE TO BANDING HEROES!

To be recognized in this way and summed up appropriately in the following article in the British Bandsman dated January 2002

Haydn Griffiths who founded Armthorpe Elmfield Band in 1964 and has served his community with countless charitable initiatives was awarded the MBE. For Haydn being honoured with the MBE was the icing on the cake which saw Armthorpe Elmfield become 3rd Section Champions and brought him an invitation to conduct Black Dyke Band. Commenting he said, 'you don't do these things in the expectation of receiving something, but I'm chuffed to bits. It's been a successful year for me. Winning the Yorkshire Regional Championship and conducting Black Dyke when I went to listen to them at Selby was absolutely marvellous, and now this on top of all that – it's just a pity that Jean my wife is not here to enjoy it.'

'What happened on the day'. A brief account from Haydn regarding being summoned to the Palace!

Haydn and son Glyn and granddaughter Anne Louise all went down to London by train. David grandson, would follow later as he had an exam to do back at school, so a taxi was arranged to take him immediately after he had finished from his school – Hunger Hill to the Railway Station. Once in London, the main party took a taxi from their Hotel to Buckingham Palace and during the drive through London the taxi driver said in all the years that he had been driving a London taxi he had never been asked to take anyone to Buckingham Palace. I suppose it's a place where London taxi drivers are requested to take foreign customers and especially those from the USA to the gates of Buckingham Palace, or on a drive past, but not actually to the Palace! Funnily enough according to Haydn when they came out of the Palace the same taxi driver was just driving past again and recognized him) and he put his thumbs up.

Inside the palace they have a practice and after assembling in a room, are put at ease with soft music playing. It was actually band music Haydn recalls – Men of Harlech, so most suitable! We then had to go through what will happen. During this time Glyn and Anne Louise had gone into the Ballroom early to secure good seats.

Haydn then goes on to say that when it was his turn he went up to Prince Charles who had obviously been briefed before the occasion so that he could have a conversation. (I asked Griff if he told him that the Band had played for his Mam and Dad when they visited Doncaster in 1977!) Charles in his conversation commented that he (Haydn) had been banding for a long time. They had quite a lengthy conversation.

When leaving one of the Beef Eaters on duty said – Hello Haydn, well done. He was a local lad from Cantley. And when they got back to the hotel a bottle of Champagne was waiting for them which the band had arranged. A fitting end to a marvellous day.

A fact that is often said is that behind a good man is usually a good woman, so it should be of no great surprise when I say that whilst I have said that 'Our Boss' the Band leader was Griff, it can also be said that the true Boss certainly in the early days, (my opinion), was Jean, Haydn's wife. A true lady in all respects, who also knew a thing or two about 'Banding Life'! Jean could and would comment critically, objectively, constructively even, and without doubt, come up with sensible suggestions for the betterment of the band. After all She had a lot of experience knowing, loving and working with a totally fanatical (excessively enthusiastic) bandsman for whom only the very best is nearly good enough.

Band Presentation to commemorate Haydn's MBE.

Mayors Parade 1ˢᵗ June 2002 with MBE medal.

This brings me to yet another little story which you will hear lots of in the course of the book, but I should mention that this next account is from the Author, but having said that, really there is no author, as there are many contributions to what has been written. Anyway, going back to my tale, I have been known to quote or make a statement in my professional life as an engineer, particularly when assessing the quality of a product or service, as being 'not bad'. This fact comes back to me, because a very old friend and someone whom I have dealt with for many years during my life on the railways – Fred Hiscock, once said to one of his employees when reporting back having done a job for me, 'how did you get on Andy'? The answer OK I think, I did this and this and got the system working again. Fred said, "Good and what did Alan say?" Employee Andy, a bit disgruntled, "er well OK – not bad." Fred said, "If Alan said it's not bad, it's good enough. Don't worry."

So, the point I am making I guess, is that Haydn's standards have 'rubbed' off on me and I am sure many others that he has had contact with over the years, so when it is said by Haydn, and/or particularly Jean, that if it is not bad, it means it's not bad, and whilst not glowing in the glory of – this is fantastic, superb, and/or absolutely brilliant, you know that the people that count and approve, are happy with the performance. Before leaving this particular topic, one might argue that standards can very often vary, depending on a level or degree of quality which is of course true, but equally so standards set by Haydn Griffiths, and enhanced by Jean his wife, can only be said to be very good, which proved instrumental to many in life's own personal experiences.

Jean once said to me when I asked her what she thought about the band, Haydn and band life in general, 'I am used to it, I am a bandsman's wife', but Jean was, a very 'strong' instrumental influence and whilst the 'Boss' would not necessarily admit it, Jean encouraged and sometimes, pre-empted, a way to go forward, and beyond. It should also be remembered that Jean did a marvellous job as mother and grandmother to a family that grew as she got older! Unfortunately, after their son Glyn's marriage breakup, Granny Jean took over looking after Anne Louise and David, and it goes without saying that both the grandchildren became active band members.

CHAPTER 8

FIRST ENCOUNTERS WITH ROYALTY

As the band developed and we became more professional and started having more tunes to play than a few hymns and the latest tune from Z Cars or Match of the Day, and /or a ballad from Ken Trinder, we engaged Geoff Downing the father of band members Nick and Chris, to provide the band with more professionalism and more importantly add quality to our concerts by effectively being compere and announcing what we would be playing.

It should be mentioned here that in those early days the band would always be the first to play the latest hit parade tune or that of any popular TV programme at the time. Tunes such as the theme tune from 'Z Cars', Match of the Day, Van de Volk, and of course when Sandy Shaw won the European Song Contest with 'Puppet on a String', they were all favourites. We even started playing the Floral dance after Terry Wogan brought it to the hit parade in 1978. Now I am told by Haydn he has over 1200 arrangements that he has prepared. That in its self must be something of a record and certainly an achievement not to be ignored.

So on with the story and when the two bands became one, the majority of band practice nights took place at Doncaster Elmfield House Youth Club on Bennetthorpe, Doncaster, where on occasions in the summer when the weather was nice we would assemble outside in the grounds to practice, and sometimes practice marching! It was on one of these occasions when 'Old Bill' (Bill Skitt), who had more than a passing interest in brass band music, was sitting in the grounds. From that initial introduction and his association with Mr Derek Webster a well-known member and 'Book Maker' of Doncaster Race Course a long and eventful relationship at the Race Course began. Amongst other benefits and possibly a more important aspect at the time was the fact that we now had another drummer to replace Sue Fletcher who had left to go to college, and then Ray Kilcoyne who left us to join the Royal Air Force. It also opened many avenues for playing at the Race Course on Race Days particularly on the 'famous' events such as the Grand St Leger which the band was fortunate to be invited to play at the 200th running of this famous 'Classic' horse race.

It can be said, interestingly, that Doncaster Race Course only two miles away from Armthorpe never featured on some people's radar so it was quite interesting to see how some of these 'horsey' folk behaved, or should I say the people that attended on race days, when we were playing. The band would be set up in a convenient place inside and ready to play during the interval. We would play various numbers but as soon as a race started everyone would put down their drinks and disappear outside shouting and cheering for their favourite horse. When the race was finished the said same people would come back in, go to the bar, get another drink and continue where they had left off with their conversations not bothering to pick up their drinks which were often barely touched. It certainly enlightened some of us in what happens at a day at the races.

Del reminds us of one occasion when we were playing in one of the boxes when some obviously distinguished guest took pity on us and lowered down a bottle of champagne and the glasses from the balcony above. Not that we touched any of it of course!

The Band enjoyed quite a lot of success from this 'chance' meeting with 'Old Bill' not least when it played at the official luncheon, held to mark the Silver Jubilee visit to Doncaster of H.M The Queen and H.R.H. The Duke of Edinburgh on Tuesday 12th July 1977. The Queen did not come out into the area (quadrangle) where we were playing because she had a cold, but Prince Phillip came out and asked Graham (Jim) Wildey how he was getting on and whether it needed a lot of puff to play the tenor horn.

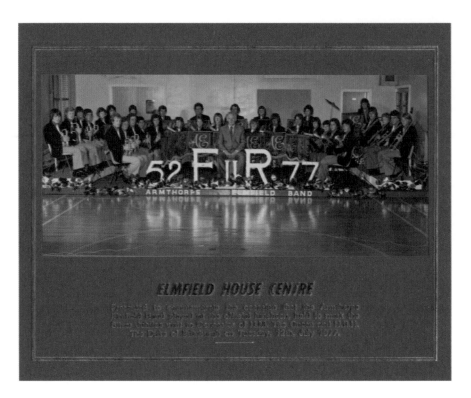

The following is taken from Newspaper Article following this occasion.

Prince lost for words.

It's not often that Prince Philip is at a loss for words … but it happened during the Royal visit to Doncaster yesterday.

During luncheon in the Tattersalls Suite the Duke was under the impression that the sweet strains of chamber music floating through the Grandstand were on tape. And he was speechless with admiration when he later learned that the musical background to the rattling cutlery was in fact, provided by the talented youngsters from Armthorpe Elmfield Youth Club.

Congratulating musical director Haydn Griffiths on the band's performance, the Duke afterwards confessed: "I honestly thought it was piped music. It sounded so professional."

Youth club organizer, Mr Ron Bailey, said: 'obviously Prince Phillip was surprised by the quality of the band and he was even more impressed to learn that the youngsters were from a youth club. It's always nice to get a pat on the back for effort but it makes it so much more satisfying when the praise comes right from the top'

Much of the credit must go to the band's mentor, Mr Griffiths, of Fernbank Drive, Armthorpe, who gives most of his free time to the club's musical activities. He is a joiner at Markham Main colliery and his family has a long musical tradition – his father was bandmaster of Markham Main band – but then, with a name like Haydn, he was always bound to strike the right note.

He is justifiably proud of the performance of his young protégés and with the Royal seal of approval as reward, it makes all those hours of hard rehearsal seem very much worthwhile.

Following on from that and as one might expect the band had many engagements for weddings, birthdays, including a special 100th Birthday (see later) funerals, garden party's special occasions, etc. which leads me into the next aspect of life in the 'Band'.

But before we go, I have to say, there you are Jim Wildey, famous!

CHAPTER 9

SPECIAL OCCASIONS

Frank Pratt as well as the many jobs in the Band also had a 'Proper' job as we say. He was a Parish Councillor for Armthorpe Parish Council and consequently had an involvement with the Band from the early beginnings and through this involvement we were asked to play at a particular Birthday Party. This pleasant occasion happened on Sunday 15th September 1974 when the Band played at Rose House Old Folks Home in Armthorpe for Mrs Margaret Fuggle's 100th Birthday. The Band regularly played at this Old Folks Home which was the only one then, bringing Christmas Cheer to both Residents and Staff so it was a great pleasure to be asked to play for some ones Centenary Birthday.

There was another occasion when the Band played to celebrate a centenary, but this was when they played in the Mappin Art Gallery in Sheffield in the presence of people like the High Sherriff of Yorkshire and the Master Cutler to celebrate the centenary of Peglers brass foundry, a local Doncaster factory famous around the world for its high-quality brass fittings.

As time went on and as mentioned earlier the Band started to participate in Entertainment Competitions and were fortunate to qualify and play at the Festival Hall in London. On this occasion, we were on the stage with the Band of the Irish Guards plus the patrons of the Boys Club of Great Britain that included His Royal Highness the Duke of Gloucester, Captain the Viscount Althorpe M.V.O., D.L, Mr Tony Kaye Vice Chairman.

This was also a competition and we were representing Elmfield House Youth Club, Doncaster. There were some very good acts and stiff competition, especially a West Indian 'Steel' Band from London, and a particularly good singer called Martin Hughes. They were all really very good, however having won Sheffield with Music from the 'Royal Fireworks' the previous year, Griff decided we should at least play that. And that was that!! Even members of the professional band stood up. The applause well, the jubilation – well, and tears even from some of the most 'hardy' members of the band. It even brought a 'tear' to Terry Elson's eye but he would never admit it.

I recall standing at the side of Griff waiting to go back on after all the acts had performed, and standing at the side of Frankie Vaughan who had just done a few songs. He would lead us back on, and sweating profusely from all the lights etc Haydn said, -you've got a bit of a sweat on 'Lad'! We had been playing in-front of some distinguished guests in the audience including The Duke & Duchess of Kent, Frankie Vaughan, Joe Bugner, Henry Cooper, Tom O'Connor, Brain Close, Derek Dougan, Ian Edwards, Arnold Long, Terry Payne, Richard Carew-Pole, Stan Stennett. All Patrons of the National Association of Boys Clubs.

Another good time had by all, but a long couple of days and because some of the Band had to take leave from School caused a bit of friction with Armthorpe Comprehensive School as it was now called which eventually led to the band becoming disassociated with the School and going its own way.

In fact, we had such a good time that Ray Kilcoyne a former member of the band and now a member of that very distinguished association the Royal Air Force came to see us play at the Festival Hall with a few of his pals. He enjoyed it so much he decided to stay the night and camped out on someone's floor. Unfortunately, he was put on a 'charge' for that when he returned to Barracks!

The Band has shared the stage with fairly important and well-known people and also played for them. We have mentioned playing for the Queen and Prince Phillip and also Princess Margaret and Duke and Duchess of Gloucester, and on another occasion, were invited to take part in a Service of Thanksgiving for the Life and Work of Olave, Lady

Baden-Powell, G.B.E. (World Chief Guide) which was performed again at Doncaster Race Course on Sunday 2nd October 1977.

The Bands increasing popularity was called upon on another occasion which was also when the R.A.F March Past was added to the repertoire was when they played in honour of Air Vice-Marshall D.B. Craig when he was chief guest at the Duke of Edinburgh's Award Scheme presentation evening at Wheatley Hills Modern School in November 1978.

Whilst talking about Entertainment Competitions we were once in a 'Local' competition which was being broadcast on Radio Sheffield and again the 'Boss' decided we would play a selection including a section from the 1812 Overture by Tchaikovsky. To make it realistic he decided to get two of the band members' father, Fred Paling, who happened to be an enthusiastic member of a Shooting Club to fire his twelve-bore shotgun at the back of the stage. Of course, these were 'Blanks' but the smoke and noise were certainly authentic and convincing! We won again, but we had some complaints from the band that followed us. Not sure why?

Ike & Tina Turner

Following our success at the Festival Hall, the following year we were invited to Liverpool to play at the Royal Theatre which was held on the 23rd November 1975. This was compared by Tom O'Connor and again had some fairly famous people who could be seen on the television. Ike and Tina Turner, Mac & Katie Kissoon, Freddie 'Parrot Face' Davis and some of the Comedians that were popular at the time, The Irish Guards and representatives from Everton and Liverpool football Club. On another occasion, the band was in the company of Dana and Michael Crawford.

It was about this time in Liverpool after playing that Sir Charles Groves was quoted as saying, 'I thought I was listening to Black Dyke'.

Mac & Katie Kissoon

Personal Management
PETER WALSH
74A Kensington Park Road
London W11 Tel. 01-727 5683

Playing in a band is often thirsty work as most bandsmen will tell you! So, at lunch time some of the older members decided to wet their whistle and went into the pub next door for a swift half. Robert (Needham) said, "It seems to be a bit busy for Monday Lunchtime," or whatever day it was? Then we found out why when some of the ladies came in with not many clothes on, and when they left they had even less on. It was quite interesting to see some of the band's parents hiding behind the pillars, but perhaps we should leave it there.

Maybe not! Whilst on this theme I have been reminded recently when we used to play for an annual event run by the 'Round Table' – you know that respectable organization of Business Men?? Well these respectable Gentlemen obviously enjoyed a 'tipple' and would have several whilst listening to the Band. There has been one thing that has always been puzzling me all this time is why some of these men had talcum powder on their lapels after the break, or was it custard powder?

Playing for other special events include playing for the Duke of Edinburgh in 1982 at Harrogate which would appear is now becoming a bit of a regular thing, and again in April the same year when we played at Liverpool's Aintree race course for the Grand National. On this occasion, the band played opposite the stands entertaining Royalty yet again.

A final remembrance for this time of year was when the Band was playing in the Dell in Hexthorpe, a traditional old bandstand which has been a very popular venue for bands in its time. On this occasion, it was in 1997 the day after Princess Diana died.

On the 31 August 1997, Diana, Princess of Wales died as a result of injuries sustained in a car crash in the Pont de L'Alma road tunnel in Paris, France. Her friend, Dodi Fayed, and the driver of the Mercedes-Benz 140, Henri Paul, were pronounced dead at the scene; the bodyguard of Diana and Dodi, Trevor Rees-Jones was the only survivor. Although the media blamed the paparazzi following the car, an 18-month French judicial investigation found that the crash was caused by Paul, who lost control of the car at high speed while drunk.

So, on this most unfortunate day, the Band was playing to a very subdued audience in very eerie conditions and as Del (Gane) said to emphasize the eeriness a thunderstorm started, and it began thunder and lightning.

CHAPTER 10

NUMEROUS WEDDINGS AND A FUNERAL

It should not take much imagination for one to realize that there have been many weddings associated with the band over the years and whilst introducing this next section another little story came to mind which will hopefully bring a smile to your face.

When I am not cutting the grass at my bungalow here in Armthorpe, I sometimes spend time trying to extend British Rail's railway lines to Dubai. I am explaining this because last September our Bangladeshi tea boy – Miraz went back to Bangladesh to get married in a 'pre-arranged' marriage, and whilst I am not saying that the marriages in the band were pre-arranged, there were quite a lot of them over the years, both between actual band members, and brothers, sisters and friends of the band. There is also a common understanding (another anecdote) when you work for the Rail Industry, as I did, it is often said that, working in the Rail Industry is an incestuous business, and so whilst I would not dare to suggest the same here in AEB, one can only wonder at the number of weddings that Griff has created?

Probably one of the first to interbreed was a trombone player and tenor horn player. Ken Trinder who as I have stated, started life as a jester and fortune teller!! and went to Danum Grammar School, and worked in banks, and in the oil Industry in Scotland, and, who according to Ken was dragged to the band by Glynis Giles who then became Mr & Mrs Trinder. Del Gane another veteran married Pom as she was always known. Pauline's mother used to manage an old folks Home in Kirk Sandal and it was a venue for our young band to play, entertaining the old people. Well it was here that romance started for Mr Gane, our tenor horn player and at 12 he was what one could call an early starter. Some of us didn't know what a girl looked like at that age? Anyway, Del and Pom another of the very first band members to get hitched is still with the band today. Del is still playing and Pauline actively supporting.

My association with a band member came about from a hospital visit made by Gillian Robinson and her brother Steve who were both in the band at the time. I was in hospital undergoing a cartilage operation and had barely come back from the operation when I could just about make out through half open eyes Gillian and Steve at my bedside. Any way after I had recovered and learnt to walk again I said to my bass mate (she played E-Flat base as I did) whilst sat on the back row that perhaps I should take her out seeing as she had visited me in hospital. Is this a common way of meeting, either visiting someone that's flat on his back in bed, or playing together on the back row? Eventually the bass's became a pair and in 1980 tied the knot to formalize the relationship which stopped the playful playing on the back row!

Chris Boyes & Helen Turner
Neil Humpheries and Julie Mawson
Liz Parke in the band, married David Prescott brother of a band member and Clarinet player at some of the earlier concerts.
Ian Robinson and Jane Gammons
Adrian Wilson and Lyn Colburn
Graham Holt and Joanne Heaton
Chris Snowden and Helen Gilden
Alan Lowe and Joanne Rimmington

Sue Fletcher, the band's first drummer.

Ken & Glynis (née Giles) Trinder September 1973

Dave & Liz (née Parke) Prescott

Del & Pom (née Wright) Gane March 1973

The Band playing for Del & Pom

Ian & Claire (née Beevor) Fairhurst

What usually follows weddings are babies and it has been mentioned that when trying to relate to a time in the past, what so often jogs the old grey matter was when a particular child was born.

During the course of growing up with the band and getting older this is exactly what happened and in some cases the baby had to come too! So, on one occasion when the band was competing in a competition and staying over in a hotel that had child intercoms (must have been a good one!) for the parents to hear should their child wake up, this was great for Steve and Annette Cunningham. This relatively new contraption was put into play which then enabled them to have a drink in the bar before going to bed because they had their baby with them and now could hear what was happening in the room.

Anyway, it was decided that Steve and Annette would have an early night and go to bed early. And guess what they forgot to turn off the intercom!! What went on in the room is a bit unclear but guess what was heard in the bar? Perhaps we should not explore that avenue any further, however it was noted that after 9 months the same couple had another baby. I wonder!!

Quite the reverse of the joyous occasion that a wedding brings, and as invariably happens when you cover a long period of time which this book is trying to do, you get the inevitable people passing away and I, was one to be affected, having lost my wife Gillian also a band member to Breast Cancer in 1991. Whilst the band did not play on this occasion the offer was made but unbeknown to me until later had been declined which was most unfortunate. Many of the Band actually attended the service in our local Church.

Another loss happened sometime before this however, which I recall having seen a newspaper cutting dated 29th July 1976. 'Colleagues of Brian Gill a 28-year-old Kirk Sandall man who died recently after an illness, are to raise money for his widow and four-year-old son with a charity concert'. I remember going to see Brian with Haydn when he was in hospital at Weston Park Sheffield but at the time I suppose that I was not aware of the end results. This of course came to me later!

The article read,

A concert at the Ki-Ki Club, is being presented by Armthorpe Elmfield Band whom Brian a well-respected percussionist in the brass band world, stepped in to help many times.

Brain was involved in music since his early teens and played with Championship Section Bands, mainly as a guest basis. Top class performers who played alongside him will appear also at the concert.'

There have been two occasions when the Band did play in such unfortunate circumstances which happened in 2000 when the Band lost two dedicated AEB members. Jean, Haydn's faithful wife passed away, as indeed did George King a player, our conversationalist, singer and stripper. (See reference of visit to Herten Germany). It was with great sadness that the band had to play for such an occasion. It was doubly difficult for Haydn as he had lost a wife and a life-long friend in George. To enhance the character of the man we are talking about in this book, I am reminded of a pact that had been made between Haydn and George (King) whereby it was agreed that whoever was the first to die, the 'other' would play the 'Last Post' at his funeral. Haydn played the last post. An emotional time for all.

More recently the band was asked to play at another funeral, again one of the old original guests of the band and a long-standing friend of Haydn's, Harald Deville. Harald passed away at the ripe old age of 90 and was sent on his way by a small ensemble of friends from AEB.

CHAPTER 11

A TIME TO REMEMBER!

This next article is from a newspaper cutting that I found dating back about 4 or five years from the present day, when Haydn was about 84. It was entitled 'Together again after all this time'.

The article reads:

'A Brass and Voices' concert in a village community centre will be a very special affair. For among those performing will be two friends reunited after more than 60 years and in the audience, will be another seven classmates.

The reunion in Armthorpe Community Centre on 24th September 2011 will take place at a concert of the Armthorpe Elmfield Band and the Brackley Male Voice Choir. It follows a meeting in Brackley, Northants, when the band played there, and musical director Haydn Griffiths met up with an old pal from the village senior school, Dennis Huby, one of the Brackley members, who he hadn't seen since he was 17. The men are now aged 84.

The event was such a success that a return concert at Armthorpe was arranged. But what Mr Huby didn't know is that Mr Griffiths had arranged for seven of their classmates to also attend, to make the reunion extra special!

This really typifies the character and attributes of the man - Haydn Griffiths and you will see more of this throughout the book.

A final surprise

A few years ago, 8 to be precise I received a telephone call from one of the band's office team, Claire Beavers who explained that the band were organising a surprise party to celebrate Haydn's 80th Birthday. This would be in the Community Centre in Armthorpe in July and would I like to come. I took the opportunity to mention John Middleton also, both as Haydn's god son and a founder member, so we both attended this memorable occasion. Tony Socket the Civic Mayor at the time together with 'Chains et al' and many other Old faces, Denis Draycott for example coming all the way from Spain where he now lives, John Middleton from Hexham and many others joined the occasion.

On the arranged day, we all met in Armthorpe Community Centre at the arranged time and waited. Any way in walks Griff to applause and accompanying 'Happy Birthday'. I often wondered how it had been kept a secret because old Griff seemed to get to know about everything (sometimes before it happened!) but apparently it has been explained just recently from Arthur whilst preparing the book, was that the date of the party coincided with Arthur's Wedding Anniversary so some 'cock and bull' story was dreamt up and Haydn was going out with Mr and Mrs Lowcock.

It was good to see some old faces from the past and some of the new people who were engaged with the band at the time.

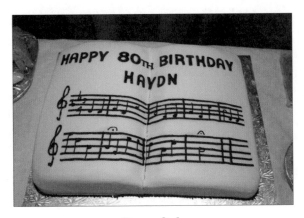

Party Cake

Baton presented by Nick Childs and Black Dyke Band

Decanter & Glasses

Old Friends reunited John Middleton, Alan Barber

Andy Pratt' Graham Wildey

Not long after this there was another celebrative occasion when the band presented Haydn with a plaque to commemorate 75 years in banding.

Band Presentation, Pocket Cornet mounted on a plinth.

A stepping stone to success

And finally, before we leave this particular section I have to say that over the years some members of the band have aspired to varying degrees of success and personal achievement.

Below are some of those:

Ray Kilcoyne left to join the RAF

Ivor Boughey started life as a Double 'B' player and finished up with Coldstream Guards.

Sarah Hickson went on to become a Major in the Army.

Adam Rosbottom played Cornet, played Ice Hockey for England.

Mick Buckley played Euphonium went on to play principal Euphonium for Brighouse and Rastrick for 13 years

Carl Ryan left to play for Grimethorpe

PART THREE

SEASONS OF THE BAND

An Ode by someone anonymous

Perhaps a fitting start to this section is this little poem titled An Ode by someone Anonymous which I found in a scrap book recently.

We are now into another year,
Last Year we had some fun
All the talented people we've met
All the contests and concerts we've done.

We've had our ups
We've had our downs
We've been through contests
First, and second rounds.

We've had our days
We've not done bad
Just think of the trophies
And medals we've had.

At Sheffield we played and won,
We enjoyed ourselves alright.
With lots of booze at back of 't' bus
We'd all thick 'eads' that night.

She starts to fuss that Mrs. G
'You ought to have known better
It's all the beer and cigs, you've had'
(Never mind, you've got to let your hair down!)

We entertained some people,
At Skegness Holiday camp,
Apart from playing instruments,
Some of us got a bit damp.

We found an outdoor swimming pool
In which we had some fun.
Some were prepared with bathing gear,
And others –like Gillian had– none!

Dragged in by so called mates
She wasn't prepared for her dipping.
And fully clothed she sank
To come out cold and dripping!

The next assignment – Blackpool
Another Competition
We had to play as never before
But finally, we'd beaten this un'.

In November, we went to Liverpool
To a National Boys Club Show
This was simply a festival
But we had a jolly good blow.

The Christmas caroling beat the lot
Around the Clubs, Pubs and Houses
The singing good, playing bad
I got beer all down my trousers.

We had some new instruments
They cost us pounds
Some members slip
They're on the ground.

Now they are full of scrapes and dints
Griff's face turns shades of blue,
It's no use doing that he hints
It wouldn't be so bad, but they're brand new.

'THEY'RE MEANT TO BE PLAYED
NOT THROWN ABOUT
I'LL TIE EM TO YA
HEAR HIM SHOUT'

The culprit's face's burning red,
'But, but I slipped, Griff,' they said
'That's no excuse, what's all the rush?'
'Well, to arrive here ready, was a push'.

The Championship section is our aim
We'd fight our way there, but it's too hard a game.
The 2nd sections just as tough
And some of us just don't practice enough.

This script is drawing to an end
And I've run out of breath
I'll have to save it for Sheffield's blow
We're not like Black Dyke yet!

The many years of solid slog,
Just to get us into practice
Our many thanks go to good old Griff
Whose taught us all our tactics!

I hope you liked this little poem by someone anonymous? I am not
sure who anonymous is but I do recognize her writing!! I think it must
relate to 1973/74

CHAPTER 12

JANUARY TO SPRING

Beginning of the Banding year

At the beginning of the year following the usually very hectic December where the Band would often be 'double' booked and on the odd occasion had to perform at three different venues, it would be time to start rehearsing for the 'Regional' finals. These would be 'Local' occasions at either Sheffield or Bradford and preliminaries for Blackpool or London, and in the early days it would be which particular one the 'Boss' wanted to go for and whether he liked the test piece. Having scoured some of the later programs it now appears that the same test piece is played at both venues, so getting two bites of the cherry so to speak and the possibility of competing in both contests.

On one occasion however, our respite over the Christmas Period was short lived because two days after Christmas Eve we were engaged to play at what is now derelict and boarded up – Doncaster Grand Theatre, (adjacent to the rear entrance of the Frenchgate Centre, and opposite the Railway Station.) It wasn't a long concert and, it got some of us out of having tea with the Grandparents!

Carrying on with the contesting 'theme' of which over the years the band has taken part in many, (see Appendix regarding the Results) it was often down to our Band Master – Haydn Griffiths whether we were successful or not. Please don't regard this as an excuse for when we did not play well nor a criticism of the Band master, but an attempt

72

to try and explain that 'Our' Master wanted the music playing his way which may not always suit everyone. So rather than a contradiction of reasoning because it was always down to him anyway, we just had to play the way he wanted us to play, and of course play well.

Contesting was a time when you had to please not only an Adjudicator, but Contesting and Entertainment Competitions, and how we played, was also about pleasing Haydn Griffiths. I have commented previously on the standards expected, but the following text hopefully enables the reader to appreciate an occasion when it did go well – very well.

If we played well and played it the way he wanted it – fine. If we didn't play well – well!! Sometimes you win, sometimes you don't, but having said that, during a regional competition at Sheffield on one occasion, the adjudicator announced the 'Runners Up', third place would go to band X, second place would go to Band Y but before announcing the winner, he went on to say 'there was only one Band who played the music as it was intended to be played' and that was – deafening applause, not sure if I heard him say the name, but everyone in the Hall seemed to know it was us. I am sure there have been similar occasions for the band but that first occasion in 1973 with 'Music for the Royal Fireworks', set the scene. This in a 'Nut Shell' summed it up, but there were many occasions when the band were acknowledged as in deed by Sir Michael Gove when he thought he was listening to Black Dyke, and again by the Duke of Edinburgh when he thought he was listening to piped music.

I have been reminded recently of an occasion in Bradford in 2001 when the opposite happened and the Band assuming that they had not done very well had gone to the bar. As Bandsman do!

There was only Chris Browne in the audience and he duly went on stage to collect the trophy. He then proceeded into the bar to let the rest know. I also understand that according to tradition the trophy was filled with beer, but unfortunately Chris in his haste to pass on the good news and enthusiasm to celebrate in the usual way failed to check the contents of the trophy. The previous recipients of the trophy had duly obliged and cleaned it before handing it back. Hence the inside still had elements of cleaning chemical/polish in it which provided a nice scum on top of the beer. (Perhaps it was Whitbread Trophy?)

Other than the participation in either of these two contests I cannot recall anything else of significance other than the odd concert and sometimes preparing for first rounds of Entertainment Competitions during the first two or three months of the year.

CHAPTER 13

APRIL THROUGH TO THE SUMMER

The tempo increases

As the year progressed and we headed towards the summer the number of engagements on our list increased, playing at the start of the summer fetes, but also taking part in the various entertainment competitions which were becoming popular at the time but it was in 1969 that we had what was probably our first proper concert, (only in the fact that there was a programme – a single sheet which we still have, stating that on Sunday 22nd June 1969 there will be a Band Concert in Warmsworth Park featuring Elmfield House Brass Band. The programme contained many of the favourite songs and tunes of the time, such as 'Puppet on a String', 'Lily the Pink' 'Trumpet Voluntary', 'Congratulations', 'When the Saints' and 'Merry Men'. And there were more so our repertoire was indeed getting bigger by now!

There was one occasion when we were booked to play at a charity concert / gala in Rossington but unfortunately it was raining and as there weren't many people to watch us, so decided to go inside and rehearse. All went well until we were about to leave and on the way out someone had put Graham (Jimmy) Wildey's instrument on the roof of Eddie Mangham's car and Eddie drove off without knowing, resulting in the instrument flying off and being run over by Mr. Prescott, one of the other parents. An example of one of many misfortunes of the band!

A story from Catherine Watson (Gilbert) remembers from the early days when Mr. Griffiths visited Edenthorpe Hall to teach music to the youngsters there, during the summer time he would get (Catherine) to run to see one of the teachers to ask for a sewing needle and then get her to remove the thorns from his fingers after he had been pruning his roses!

Mention has been made in the previous section about playing for H.M The Queen and H.R.H The Duke of Edinburgh in July 1977 but the band also played for another member of the Royal family on the 6th June 1976. The Band played in what was then called the 'Arndale' Centre which is now Frenchgate Centre. It was for Princess Margaret who was visiting Doncaster, amongst other 'things' I remember playing 'Aint She Sweet' which would of course have been another piece specially arranged by Haydn.

In fact, as you will learn during the course of the book Armthorpe Elmfield Band has played for Royalty on numerous occasions. An article I retrieved from the Internet, Royal Visit to Thorne, Thursday 3th September 2004.

Band's eye view!

HRH The Duke of Kent K.G. attended the re-dedication of the refurbished War Memorial in Thorne Park by the Bishop of Doncaster. The Mayor of Thorne greeted the Duke of Kent, The Lord Lieutenant of South Yorkshire and other guests at the entrance to the Park and then proceeded to the bandstand where invited persons were presented.

There was a parade down Church Street, round the Market Place, along Silver Street and down South Parade to the Park and then proceeded along a marked route in front of the bandstand where The Duke of Kent took the salute.

What an occasion for the band to be at, and as said, one of many for AEB. See reference later (Autumn) when Royalty visited Thorne again.

It was also a time when our Band had their own function raising money for its much-needed band funds, and Mr. Paling who had two sons in the band at the time, and owned a rather splendid house (known as the White House) in Armthorpe which had substantial gardens, so it was to be utilised! Being 'Self Financing', the band was always struggling for money, so it was decided that we would have our own event, with the band playing of course but on occasions having other acts to join us, or demonstrations. So never short of ideas Griff decided that we would have a 'Hot Dog' Supper, hence for several years, courtesy of Fred and his wife Barbara, we took over their very nice garden and effectively created a very nice garden party.

I feel that we should explain a little about exactly what the Hot Dog Supper was, apart from a money raising function. Basically, it was a garden party for the people of Armthorpe and surrounding areas. It would not be possible to mention all the activities that we had but to name some of the more interesting features which you perhaps don't get at your conventional garden parties. You could take a flight on an Arial Runway, go on a roundabout, smash the plate, get your own back by drenching someone on the ducking stool, hook a fish, try to win on the coconut- shy (of which Graham Thorpe, a band member, won four from his five balls!) or see how good a shot you were on the firing gallery which was created by using the back of Jack Smith, the local pop man's lorry. Then there was the pony ride, and we sometimes had demonstrations, such as a trampoline display from Elmfield House.

It was on one of these occasions when preparing and organizing the annual event that Griff decided we should get Kevin Keegan to join us. After all he was born in Armthorpe probably not more than a couple of hundred metres from the White House. So, we had Kevin at the 'Hot Dog' Supper who just so happened to be playing for Liverpool and England at the time, and was Captain of both. (Unfortunately, he wasn't good enough for Doncaster Rovers!!)

Born in 32 Elm Place not a stone's throw from the 'Comp' (Comprehensive School) formally Armthorpe High School the founding place of the Band and only the distance of a corner kick to the FE (Further Education) Block which was positioned in front of the school – the home of the band for the last 25 years it would have been very convenient for him to come to the band if he hadn't started messing about with footballs. He could have left home at 6.59pm for a start of band practice at 7.00 pm and still arrive with time to spare.

Local boy made good –
Kevin Keegan

In actual fact Kevin lived in Spring Gardens in the middle of Doncaster for a while which was not too far from what we called the 'New Baths' (St James Baths) and also now the new Cast Theatre where the Band will be enjoying the company of Black Dyke Band sometime in the near future who will be helping to 'fund' raise for the new band hut.

At the age of 15 Kevin was a member of Elmfield House Youth Club which would have been about the time we were starting to attend the Youth Club for band practice. It was in 1966 (an all that!) that he and 2 friends completed a run for charity from Nottingham to Doncaster.

Just think if he hadn't been kicking about with that football he could have been playing 'Match of the Day' instead of playing **in** match of the Day! Also, when he first left school he started work at Pegler's Brass Works as a clerk in the Central Stores which would have been good for him 40 years on, and a reminder of when the band played at the company's centenary. These are only a couple of coincidences of which you will read of many through- out the book.

Anyway, he turned up in a rather big posh white car which one could say didn't exactly blend into the background, so it was suggested that it be parked out of sight behind Arthur Belk's house across the road on Mere Lane and a local supporter of the band. Kevin sat on the back row at one point with the bases for photos and reckoned to be playing but he wasn't really!

It was also usual to have marching competitions and parades at the start of the summer period. These would take place around Whitsuntide, which is now Spring Bank towards the end of May, and of course the May Day holiday break had not been invented then. You will see reference to such practices and activities later in the book.

CHAPTER 14

SUMMER THROUGH TO AUTUMN

Playing in the park

Always plenty to do, as we all know that in summer time in many of the mining villages that once surrounded Doncaster, bands played at the miner's welfare grounds and parks. This time of year, also created havoc with half the band suffering from the dreaded 'hay fever'. Glyn included, the band masters son and principal cornet player. Sunglasses on, (shades as they are referred to in today's modern language) hankies at the ready, streaming eyes and wheezing – if playing on grass wasn't bad enough! I am sure that we must have a picture somewhere showing the band playing in the welfare grounds with members of the front row wearing glasses and resembling the mafia!

This is taken from a Newspaper Article I have from the Epworth Bells and Crowle Advertiser dated 15/06/1990 (and must stress it was not written by me) which states that public demand in Epworth has made a visit by the talented Armthorpe Elmfield band an annual event and so an almost full St Andrews Church greeted musical director Haydn Griffiths and his gifted players.

After an introduction from the Rev Arthur Makel, resident MC Frank Pratt (one of many jobs that Frank had in the band) did a splendid job of linking the pieces with anecdotes and light banter.

The Article goes on:

A stentorian rendering of the well-known hymn, 'O Worship the King', was enhanced by the added Double B euphoniums. The tune 'Hanover' is well known to all church goers and one could sense the desire of many of the audience to break into song. A march to warm up the instruments followed and Rossini's overture to the opera Tancrede was a golden opportunity to show off the enormous variety of sound that the band was capable of.

Next followed a piece introduced as Argentinian, but to me it certainly felt very much like Strauss, and this was underlined as the strains of 'When you are in love, it's the happiest night of the year' came through.

The first of the soloists was Christopher Boyes who on the euphonium gave a beautiful rendering of the evocative 'Watching the Wheat'. The applause he engendered brought forth an encore and for this he was joined by his talented wife Helen who, taking the soprano line on cornet, played the exciting Lloyd Webber duet 'All I Ask of You' from Phantom of the Opera.

I am told which the audience or author of this write up did not know was that Helen had been in hospital until the previous day.

Bert Kaemfert's 'Strangers in the Night' was the band's next offering and played in rhumba royale style. It proved to be quite popular.

The Air from The Handelian Suite was followed by Siebergs Hawaiin Samba which thrilled many with its rhythmic 4 4 beat. "The Clog Dance', written by a Yorkshireman, with the unlikely name of John Mark Angelo, was the band's next offering and was well received, although Frank Pratt, while introducing the following number suggested that clog dancing at that speed was nigh impossible. The number he was announcing was another Lloyd Webber piece 'Love Changes Everything' – quite beautiful.

More rhythm from Seiberg, Hawaiian Hoe Down, followed before we were honoured with the presence again of the band's solo cornetist Helen Boyes who thrilled all with a beautiful rendering of 'Bless This House' and 'Somewhere Over The Rainbow'.

For me, the highlight of the evening says the writer of this, was Mascagni's Easter Hymn: Armthorpe and Elmfield band really did this full justice. The harmonies were heard to full effect and the whole rousing performance moved the audience to sustained applause.

Gustav Holst's March from his Second Symphony in 'F' Major thrilled all the audience before moving into a quite splendid tribute to Lionel Bart's 'Oliver'. This is certainly one of the most favourite musicals and the audience were encouraged to sing – and they did. The more than generous applause brought the absolute finale the wonderful old hymn 'Guide Me O Thou Great Redeemer' to which the audience gave full voice.

I don't think you could get a more complimentary resume of the bands playing even if it had been written by a band member!

A similar accolade was written for a similar concert In Epworth in June 1988 also announcing the attributes of the band and regular visitors to Epworth Agricultural Show Day. We have further references to these particular concerts in Epworth with stories from Catherine Gilbert later.

Personally, I am pleased to hear that the band still enchants audiences with the Easter Hymn, I remember when we first played it which was a couple of years prior to 1980, and as I was getting married on Easter Saturday (to a band member) such an occasion would be enhanced by this Hymn. The music was played after the church service but unfortunately not by the band, because as you will hear later, they were returning from Germany – which would be the first of many foreign visits, and Gillian not as optimistic as myself preferred to 'edge' on the safer side!

CHAPTER 15

AUTUMN THROUGH TO CHRISTMAS

Final race to Christmas

Always the busiest time of year, rehearsing for one of the 'finals'. Blackpool was always a favourite because it was in early November and the Blackpool Illuminations etc. were in full swing. We would always go to the venue the night before, but 'Griff' had a strict policy to adhere to before contests which particularly was aimed at the older ones and no alcohol! On one occasion however, when we were at Blackpool, we couldn't all get in the one Hotel and a few of the older members had to stay in the nearby Imperial Hotel across the road. I seem to remember another good time had but we'll say no more about that and don't tell the Old Man!

One of our members came from outside of Armthorpe and a bit 'posh' played Golf at Wheatley Golf Club that happened to have an association with a Golf Club in Heysham. We would then on the Sunday leave Blackpool to travel to Heysham Golf Club for a lunch time concert. Always a good occasion and always a full bus of band and supporters. A good weekend, but not always for some of the band!

Following on from Blackpool which was often just before bonfire night, we would return to play on the back of a local coal lorry, playing around the village and culminating in playing at the actual bonfire. I am told that on one of these occasions a trombone slide falling off. Maybe Andrew can elaborate?

As mentioned previously if the band did well in the Regional's they would progress to either Blackpool of London. The above is the account of Blackpool and often on occasions when they went through to London it would be in Hammersmith because only the top section bands actually made it to the Albert Hall however in 1995 the band was fortunate to play in the Royal Albert Hall. What a fantastic experience – what Bandsmen dream of!

Old folks Christmas concert

The article below taken from a Local Armthorpe Magazine in 2014 emphasizes the continued popularity of the band and busy schedule they have leading up to Christmas.

The Armthorpe Elmfield Band has been busy in the village recently. They played at the Miners memorial service at the beginning of September, and 2 weeks later played for the RAF parade through the village to the church for service of remembrance.

The same weekend saw the band on parade in Adwick for a church celebration. At the end of the month they were in action in Rossington to raise money for the Rossington Scouts as one of their members, who also plays in the band is travelling to Japan in 2015 for the world scout jamboree. £350 was raised for this and a very entertaining evening was enjoyed by the audience. The junior band was also on the stage and received good applause. It is important to support our up and coming members of the band, as who knows where their talent will lead them.

On October 10ᵗʰ the Doncaster German Society and friends of Herten held their annual Oktoberfest at the Ukrainian Club in Doncaster. The band played traditional German Songs and everyone enjoyed a bit of Bavaria as we were transported to the Hofbrauhaus in Munich for beer, sausage and song!

Going back to the Band's association with Royalty on Wednesday 12ᵗʰ October 2005 yet another Royal Member visited Thorne – this time the Princess Royal opened a new footbridge over the canal. Ken Trinder a man of many talents as we have heard is a professional photographer and on the said day was duly obliging. Ken tells me that he was doing a similar thing, carrying out official' photographic duties in 2000 when he lived in Aberdeen when Princess Anne visited a Victim Support Centre in Inverurie and it was by coincidence in 2005 that one of Princess Anne's same body guards was there and remembered Ken and spoke to him.

The Princess Royal meets Haydn at Thorne

Following on from this appointment with Princess Anne in Thorne the band were asked to play another engagement at Fishlake where they were opening the Church that had been refurbished, and were obviously surprised to see again the Princess Royal. Maybe she liked it so much that she wanted to hear them again!

The Princess moves on to Fishlake, and the band were already there to play her in.

CHAPTER 16

MARCHING A WAVERING TRADITION!

One aspect of banding is marching which used to be a regular event for brass bands that appears to be in a somewhat decline these days. However, our band continues to maintain the tradition especially at this time of year, so from the early days of marching in the grounds of Elmfield House, 40 years later we see that AEB is regularly sort after to continue these traditional and special occasions which is confirmed below.

Armistice Parade Armthorpe

Armistice Parade Burghwallis

Mayors Parade Doncaster

Global Warming March

Crowle Catholic Parade

In November, last year (2014) the band had a busy remembrance weekend as they paraded through the village for the annual service of Remembrance at the local Church of St Mary & Leonard's in the Village, followed by lunchtime parade and service for the Royal British Legion in Burghwallis, and then performing at their annual concert in Doncaster.

Well I think it is time to mention a little story about 'Marching' that now takes place, and as said AEB is probably one of the last remaining bands in the area to march and as can be seen from these articles are still very active in this and in great demand. Unfortunately, not all the members are as fit as they used to be and sometimes the bass drum from which they get their 'beat' is pushed in a super market trolley!

There was also an occasion I am reliably advised where the leader of the pack was escorted by soldiers who ably assisted and provided a helping hand, and I am also told of an occasion when the leader of the band was actually riding in a police car. I wonder what that could be about!

Perhaps we will learn later?

I have also been advised of other marching stories when the band took part in Greenfields Village Marching competition around the Saddleworth Area. The Bands have to visit all the local villages where they are judged 'marked' not only on their playing but also marching. This takes place around Whitsuntide so therefore in May and if you are really lucky you may even see a band practicing in the middle of the moors?

Anyway, to continue, as I said it is not uncommon for the band to have three engagements on one day and here is evidence of that. Later that same evening having been on two different marches the band held its annual celebrity concert at the Earl of Doncaster Hotel. The guest player was Richard Marshal, principle cornet player of the world famous Black Dyke Band. Richard is a local man and his early years learning to play cornet were here in Doncaster. In October the Black Dyke Band were crowned champions again at the National Brass Band finals (2014) at the Royal Albert Hall in London.

Armthorpe Elmfield Band were delighted to be able to bring Richard's talent to Doncaster for an amazing evening of music and entertainment celebrating Remembrance Sunday with a mixture of poppies and patriotism. The junior band also featured in this concert, and it was a pleasure to hear them play some traditional and modern tunes, from Elvis to One Direction.

Over the years the band has participated in many concerts where a 'Guest' player from a well 'known' band would join us on stage. It was not uncommon to have a cornet player or euphonium player sat amongst the band that had come from Brighouse and Rastrick, Brodsworth or even Black Dyke. Below are but a few.

Chris Jeans	Black Dyke
James Sheppherd	Black Dyke
Chris and Helen Williams	Fodens
Roger Webster	Black Dyke, Brighouse & Rastrick, Grimethorpe
Michael Dodds	Grimethorpe
Richard Marshall	Black Dyke
David Dixon	Grimethorpe (once played with the Band having just returned from Australia touring with his band – Grimethorpe Colliery Band)

Haydn with James Shepherd in the band room

Other examples of accompanists to the Band include:

Anston male Voice Choir with Chris Jeans, Principle Trombone player, and Tony Capstick . 29th October 1995.

Castleford male Voice Choir with Simon Johnson on Trombone and Tony Capstick. 20th September 1998.

Helen Fox, Principle Cornet and Tony Capstick. 19th April 1998

Doncaster ladies Choir, with David Childs Euphonium Virtuoso. 25th March 2000

Shearing's Featherstone Male Voice Choir with James Shepherd Cornet Virtuoso

Scunthorpe Male Voice Choir, with Simone Rebello, Percussionist. 23rd September 2000

Destelm Backam Spielmannzug Band (Herten). 31st May 2002

Worrell Male Voice Choir with Michael Dodd Principal Euphonium. 8th September 2007

Castleford Male Voice Choir with Helen Fox (Cornet) and Glyn Williams Vituoso Euphonium. 5th July 2008.

Shearing's Featherstone Male Voice Choir with Roger Webster on Cornet. 30th May 2009.

The band as you have heard has shared the stage with many well- known celebrities which you will be introduced to throughout the book, some were playing 'themselves' and perhaps not fully communicating with the band, whilst others actively joined in, taking part, pretending to conduct or whatever. I remember Charlie Williams well known on television and of course being from Barnsley being one of the friendly ones. I think he took over conducting from Haydn at one point.

As I said at the start of this section December was always busy in the run up to Christmas, and here is a typical example of engagements during in the run up to Christmas performing at the local Christmas Fayre on 29th November, Thorne Parish Church on 5th December, In the Eagle and Child public house on 9th December, local Community Centre on Saturday 13th December for the Senior Citizens, December 14th Christmas Joy Concert, Christmas Draw on 17th December, and of course then the regular 'carolling' which has being undertaken since the bands infancy.

A Song to celebrate the happenings in a year

So on that note, we will finish as we started but this time with a little song from someone anonymous which tells us some more about the years events.

We've had our ups and had our downs
We've been through contests many around
We've had out days and not done bad
Just think of the Trophies and Medals we've had.

Chorus

When we're in the Band room
There's only one in charge
There's no need to say who that is,
He's rather bald and large!

We went to Skeggy for a little trip
Some of us decided to take a dip.
The ones with costumes enjoyed the camp
The rest of us came home very very damp.

Chorus

She starts to fuss that Mrs G_ _ _
You'd have done better if you'd listened to me,
Now we know why he's bald and grey,
Griff tells us She nags him night and day.

Chorus

Florrie and Eddy are a lovely pair,
Of the kids they take good care.
The girls all say He's rather good looking,
But he messed us about with a double booking.

Chorus

Christmas comes but once a year.
Just as well cos we're on the beer!
They say there's a shortage of drinking glasses.
But we know where they are. They're at Alan's Old Lasses!

Chorus

Del and Pom are expecting an event
Dell must have tried an experiment
They don't even know what it's names gonna be,
But Griff's got it down for a Double 'E'

Chorus

And now we have come to the end of our tale,
As Mr. Griffiths calls it, Our Finale.
We don't really mean what we have said,
And as Zebedee says 'It's time for bed'

So as a final 'finale' to this section I make reference to trying to remember the dates of an event or occurrence which is usually helped by a family or personal event or date in one's life to jog the old memory cells. I mention this because I am continually reminded when I get together with some of the band members and we are trying to remember something, a particular date of a concert or contest, that it was such and such a time – our so and so was born in 1986 so it was around then, or whatever it was. Regarding the above little song, Del and Pom had their first child a boy on 9th February. Chris Boyes however is different, he says "I'm terrible with dates, I remember 'Test Pieces'. "

Is he the 'anorak' of banding? (A term used for Train Spotters!)

PART FOUR

PRELUDE – LET THE *'TALES'* BEGIN

Some early Stories from the Band

As we travel through time that the Band has been in existence the journey has sometimes been difficult as no doubt you will have realized, but what I can say is that along with the difficult times we had plenty of good times. The next section is a selection of little stories from band members which hopefully enables the reader to appreciate the fun and enjoyment we had bringing enjoyment to 'Others'. So, read it and please accept it as it is, laugh with us laughing at ourselves as we recall the memories.

Laugh with us, and we will laugh with you!

But first, we have to get to where we are going, so the first part of this section is a selection of short stories from the happenings on the bus.

CHAPTER 17

ON THE BUSES!!!

So first, getting there, and whilst it appears repeating the references that have been made elsewhere in the book regarding the support we were fortunate to have from parents, friends and relatives, and particularly those who regularly joined us on our journeys, were also part of the band and where we went they came too. So this is like a little tribute to all our friends over the years, so let's get going with the interesting section which also provides you with a little 'insight' to our days away!

As a way of introducing this part can I remind some of the readers that may remember the popular TV programme with Reg Varney and Robert St Claire Grant 'On the Buses' and the pranks they got up to. Whilst we did not have Reg Varney and Bob Grant, we did have some interesting times, whether it be our 'resident' on board mechanic Bob Needham who occasionally had to get involved with breakdowns in order to get us to the concert or contest, the antics of band members, all of which were invariably keeping the supporters entertained. So, with no further ado and to coin another regular phrase expressed from 'Our Leader' keep one eye on Me, one eye on your Music and one eye on your pocket, so taking note of that, lets continue reading with a few stories of times 'On the Buses'?

Carryings On – 'On the Buses' shall we say?

This first story really goes back to the very early days when the band started to visit Blackpool for the day which was before we ever started to compete, and it was on one of these occasions in 1968 that two enterprising band members decided to complement their mediocre income. One, an apprentice plant fitter from the railway and someone who was just about to go to college in Newcastle decided they would buy some beer from the 'off licence' at the Tadcaster Arms, known locally as the 'Taddy'. On the said Friday night after band practice, the two entrepreneurs took their plastic water carrier to the off licence and had it filled with beer. Part one of the plan executed!! The problem now was that neither of the pair dare take the beer home, so it was hidden under the hedge at the bottom of Mr. Palin's garden, i.e. at the bottom of the garden where we had the 'Hot Dog' Supper, after all it was at the Taddy that we would be picked up at 06.30am the following morning and directly opposite the White House.

Alan, clip board in hand, organising things on the bus, or possibly taking beer orders!

One might say that the journey to Blackpool became more interesting and entertaining as time went on, (to some anyway) but it did get a little less enjoyable for those who became desperate for the loo.

I think a suitable profit was made selling it at 6d (2.5p in new money) per cup (plastic)

Another little story before we get on with some of the contributions by 'others' happened to me on one occasion whilst travelling on the bus. I have a capped tooth not exactly my front teeth but the next one along. This was acquired during my Rugby days at Doncaster. Anyway, for some unknown reason (unless we had an emergency brake application) it decided to fall out on the way to some concert or contest or whatever. First job was to find it so after some time spent on hands and knees I came up triumphantly having found it, only to be met by 'All I want for Christmas is a new front tooth". Well it was towards the end of the year and not long before Christmas.

Robert recalls that on one of the occasions the Band went to Germany, first the driver got lost in Aachen, and then him taking a little snooze (power nap I think they are called in today's modern world) but whilst he was driving. So, Robert as well as being the on-board mechanic also had to keep the driver awake. He finishes his story by saying some lucky people actually flew. Not sure who they were but one was the band secretary and Florrie his wife and the other couple was the Man in the Middle and Jean. Lucky Bruges is what I think Robert said!

Michael Buckley a member of the band for many years who eventually went to play for some band called Brighouse & Rastrick or other and a very good euphonium player was also good at playing tricks and getting into trouble, but all part of growing up. Without divulging too much there has been occasions when the said young man finished up stripped of his clothes (this was the fore runner to George King who joined the Band later and was good at singing and stripping). I am reminded of one occasion when Mick got stripped and all his clothes were thrown to the front of the bus. Unfortunately, Mr. Griffiths was following in his car. He was not a happy bunny, as they say!

Then there was another occasion when Mick tried to get off the bus only to find he had his shoe laces tied together. I think Jim had crawled under the seats to achieve that.

He was compensated when everyone sang Happy Birthday outside the bus on one of our first visits to London. Mick was I believe the first member of the band to own his own instrument, a euphonium. Michael got a Saturday job on Doncaster market on one of the many butcher's stalls in the indoor part. He saved all his money so that he could purchase his own instrument. At least no one could claim to own that and take it back from us! Working on the butcher's stall also gave Haydn another reason to make comment at the way we played sometimes. He used to say we played just like a sausage machine which they used to fill with mince and bread and endless other rubbish and mince it all up to make a sausage, and you sound just like that!

Mick Buckley's birthday, happy birthday being played by Richard Boyes, his brother Steve singing lustily, Haydn and Eddie Mangham looking on.

It was an exciting time going to London then, as some of the band members had never ventured that far. I remember taking Terry (Elson) and some of the older ones on a tour of the Underground. We covered all the Stations on the monopoly board without getting out once, so it cost us about 6p.

It did not take long before the band having gained in numbers and popularity it was only natural that the 'Boss' had us competing in more contests, initially in the Regional events (Bradford or Sheffield) and if we did well would then go on to compete at Blackpool Winter Gardens or London. It was on one of these occasions coming back from Blackpool when we were involved in a crash on the motorway – a car ran into the back of the bus. Nearly all the instruments were damaged in some way, especially Robert Needham's double 'B' which finished up with a flat bell end. There are several stories relating to mishaps with buses, and 'break down' like unable to get the gears, but 'we' sorted that one says Robert. Then there was the time when we had a puncture in one of the front tyres. We had a spare wheel but no jack. Robert recalls we went into Saddleworth got a jack, and changed the wheel then went onto Broadhurst for the concert.

Steve Cunningham and Del Gane, serious as ever

Before we move on, getting off the bus so to speak, I must mention Bob the stalwart of the Bass section who additional to his contributions to 'Merry Men' he was sometimes called to undertake some mechanic-ing and Mr. 'Fix it' could be relied upon to get us to the Church on time, and other times when returning home. He also became what we might call an early navigation system when the driver got hopelessly lost.

In recalling Robert's stories which in one aspect we were very lucky, and no one was hurt in these accidents / incidents, on the other hand it shows how unfortunate we have been forever facing an uphill battle.

I suppose though that we were in a way fortunate to have so many comedians in the band that took us through the early years bringing laughs and merrily helping along the way. And who were those four or five that did a moony on the bus?? Will we ever know I say? But what we have found out whilst researching the book is that Andrew's Mum and Dad (Joan and Frank) had a camera so it was all recorded on film, and any way Mrs. Pratt said I can recognize who's who!

CHAPTER 18

WHATEVER HAPPENED THEN!

Now after the antics on the bus – getting there, we continue with the story and it should be said that this section is really a prologue in that it does not intend to extol the virtues of the Band to the Reader just a narrative and introduction of some of the many happy times and fond memories.

Going back then to when the band started it would be true to say that during the first 3 or 4 years we were only a Junior Band playing a few concerts here and there for the School, Old Folk's Christmas Party and perhaps the odd Church concert and the like, and as the older ones were still only 13 and 14 there was not too much to report. However, as one will appreciate it doesn't take long for the older members to grow out of their short trousers (and in fact some of the more mature ones even started growing whiskers) so by the time they reached 16 could sometimes be convincing enough to get a pint of beer in a pub. Two of the earlier proponents of this indeed would have been John Middleton and myself, (but don't tell Griff!). We would catch the bus into Doncaster on our way to Elmfield House for the practice and on the way, would call in at the 'Turf Tavern' for a pint of Barnsley Bitter.

As mentioned earlier one of our first concerts which attracted a little publicity was the one in Warmsworth Park in 1969 only in the fact there was an official programme.

It was around 1970 when we played our first contest which was in Middlesbrough. Visiting Middlesbrough in about 1970 around 45 years ago is a long time ago and the only thing that has been mentioned is that we played 'Beautiful Britain. I am guessing that the oldest members of the band would be then 18 years old.

The Band over the years has taken part in over 100 Contests either Regional, Finals or Entertainment competitions / contests the results of which can be seen at the back of the book, but as said at the start of this part it is introducing you to Armthorpe Elmfield Band from the beginning sharing with you the many memories enjoyed by members of the band and those associated with it.

It has been explained in other parts of the book about the Regional Competitions which brought about weekend visits should the band do well. You have also heard of few escapades that certain members got up to, for example when Michael Buckley lost his clothes yet again but this time in a lift! At a hotel in Blackpool Mick was devoid of his clothes in the lift of all places. The lift went up and down, up and down with Mick still in, only on one occasion during his ascents and descents it stopped and who should get in but Mrs. Wilson.

I don't know if it was a way of Jim Wildey avoiding the issue, but it was also reported that he himself was undertaking a little Spiderman antics and was seen walking along a ledge outside of the hotel, but this ledge was 4 stories up!

Whilst getting to where we are, we have sometimes mentioned a story which may have been linked to other stories relating to the memory or in some cases as a way of introducing something, a memory, a topic or occurrence. So, we will now delve into the past a little and to coin a phrase often used these days, this is not exhaustive it is merely an assembly of articles, stories and anecdotes reflecting the memories we have of Armthorpe Elmfield Band.

An early memory that relates to this era and worthy of a mention before getting into the true International adventures of the Armthorpe Elmfield Band happened in October 1972 when the band once went to Amsterdam. The intention was that we would be playing a concert. Mr. Mangham, the parent of Eddie one of the trombone players, and Senior Manager with a well-known Tractor Manufacturer in

Doncaster, International Harvesters, and, Secretary of the Band had arranged for us to give some sort of concert somewhere in Amsterdam. Great we said (particularly the older ones), only for some of the more respectable and sensible folk to say, I don't think so, bearing in mind the publicity Amsterdam was getting from the popular television program – 'Van de Volk', - legalized drugs, prostitution and sex shops etc. We did not play but we did go to Amsterdam. According to resourced information, an article taken from Gillian's scrap book, this was a 'thankyou' for the efforts that had been put in recently raising money to buy instruments.

The Band's first overseas adventure, all ready to head to the ferry at Immingham en route to Amsterdam.

So, the intrepid travellers set off from Armthorpe on the way to Amsterdam and the overnight crossing was what one might call 'rough', with just about everyone on our trip being sea sick. I remember sitting in the bar at a table with pints of beer in front of us (only the adults of course) when there was a rather large swell and twelve pints of beer finished up on the floor. What a waste!

On the short coach journey into Amsterdam bearing in mind we had sailed to Amsterdam not Rotterdam, everyone was relating their own version of events, and who had been sick. Of course, Terry had not been sick, but I remember him looking for 'hooey'!

I don't have any great stories from the day in Amsterdam, the usual 'sights'??, and a few beers in bars along the canals. I do remember some scantily clad ladies dressing up shop windows. I am not sure what they were doing but there did seem to be rather a lot of them! I also remembered going for a drink in a Scottish Bar though which was on a corner and on the main canal leading to the famous bridge which is always shown on pictures of Amsterdam. Anyway, you were given a yellow card which you had to put on your drink if you left it for a while. It said Please don't touch gone for a 'P'. I think it was Dutch for I have waited over 20 minutes for this glass of beer (because they keep taking the frothy head off with a spatula) and I don't want it taking away whilst I am visiting the WC which in this instance was an open grate at the side of the canal. The Pissoire as they were known was in view of everyone in the Pub, so you could keep an eye on your pint anyway. So, adopting one of Griff's earlier phrases, you keep an eye on what you are doing, come in at the right places and, keep an eye on your back pocket – Your beer in this case!

One final comment from Del regarding the crossing going out, he said apart from the flooded toilets due to excessive amounts of sick swashing around the floor was that all he remembered was a record that the DJ continually played, that or his needle was stuck.

There were no problems on the return trip. The North Sea as can often happen, and I have travelled it many times was as flat as a pancake, no witnessing of 12 pints flying across the table to be deposited on the floor, no undue 'greenness' in people's complexions, and no looking for 'hooey'.

Another story of this time relates to a visit to a 'fancy' house in Flaxton near York playing at a Garden party. It must have been fancy because they didn't have garden parties in people's houses in Armthorpe (except the Hot Dog Supper), and they certainly didn't have tennis courts. So here we were at this rather 'posh' place and some bright spark in the band thought it a good idea to jump over the net.

This came to an end when someone didn't quite make it which caused the net to break. Ken remembers not so much the tennis court incident but a game where there were numerous pegs on a washing line and you had to see how many you could get in one hand. Apparently according to Ken, I won because I had the biggest hand!

The audience suffering on 'prickly' straw bales at Flaxton

The time of our next little story was around 1974 and 75 when the band was invited to go to a well-known holiday camp at Skegness to put on a concert and entertain the Old Folks and Pensioners who tended to visit the camp at the back end of the Summer season.

I seemed to think that what was probably the first occasion that we were invited I had just been discharged out of hospital from having an operation to remove my cartilage, thanks to playing too much rugby, which in Griff's eyes was seen to be a distraction from my obligation and commitment to the Band. (There was to be a further distraction a few years later when I got married to Gillian, but I will come to that later).

So here I was only just discharged from Doncaster Royal Infirmary and still on crutches and certainly not able to walk, having to accept the fact that Skeggy was a no goer. However, Mr. Griffiths on the other hand had other ideas. He came to see me and said, not a problem, we can sit you on the back seat of the bus, put a cornet case in the aisle and you can sit with your leg on that, "job done". The bus pulled up right outside the house, and I only had to walk on my crutches from the front door and onto the bus.

The journey went as usual, with the usual antics by the band at the back of the bus, keeping the supporters entertained as you have just heard. Anyway, when we arrived at Skegness somebody went off to get a wheel chair (after all there should not be a shortage of such equipment being Pensioners fortnight). So, we finished up with the wheel chair and with no shortage of volunteers to push it around, with no problems that is, until Terry Elson decided to give it a go. Terry built like a bull, hard as nails, no emotions (see note at Festival Hall) said come here let me give him a real shove. It was certainly an entertaining one because no sooner had he taken control of the wheel chair one of the front wheels came off, and I finished up in a heap on the floor with my leg sticking upwards. It could only have happened to Terry, everyone is rolling around laughing whilst I am trapped under the wreckage of a collapsed wheel chair.

Another occasion I seem to recall, a good time was had by all, but the main thing I really remember is that it was a very nice hot day, so

The band at Skegness

109

much so, (and probably encouraged by Griff, (but he did not go in himself) several of the band members finished up going for a swim in the pool, Gillian (who finished up Mrs. Barber) included, but of course we had not gone prepared for such frivolity so it was down to the undies. See reference in poem at commencement of section 3.

Memories are often what one recalls over time, 'do you remember the time when', or, when did we go to? As a consequence of some of such early happenings and occurrences, certain memories that do come to 'mind' and for whatever reason, became a regular occurrence. For example, during the early days, and after a usually very busy December with many engagements, the Band would go carolling. If we were invited to the Golf Club or a particular Pub in the 'run' up to Christmas any collections / payment would go into the band funds but on Christmas Eve the takings would be divided up and distributed to Band members. Alan Humphries the Band Treasurer in the beginning would be busy counting it all in on the back of the bus whilst we did the 'rounds' of especially important houses where we were expected to be at a certain time, which often resulted in a fiver going in the box which was a lot in those days. It should be noted however that we did not always have a bus to take the band round certainly not initially. In fact, it was during these early days that as you will regularly hear, we relied very much on the support and help from parents and friends. During those first times when we ventured out on Christmas Eve we finished up back at Fred and Barbara Palin's house (White House) in the centre of Armthorpe whilst the money was being counted. Mr. Paling reminded me earlier of this whilst reminiscing along with his son Derek, he said, 'Can you remember when you came to my house the first time you ever went carolling on Christmas Eve', we had band members everywhere, sat on stairs, in the hall way, kitchen etc all waiting in anticipation as to what they may receive as a Christmas gift!

The night would start by walking the streets playing in front of houses where band members lived, (see note previously playing outside of Haydn's fathers house) then at about 19.30 we would start visiting the Pubs and Clubs of Armthorpe and the surrounding villages. Obviously on Christmas Eve all of them full to capacity. We occasionally had to wait at the side while finishing a game of Bingo, but then there were benefits especially for the older ones (and sometimes not so old!!) as several of the members had started work, at the colliery, railway and 'local' factories it was invariable that you would see someone you knew who would thrust a pint of beer into your hand (and into other places sometimes!!) Robert also remembers on one occasion when he found his Double 'B' particularly difficult to blow, only to find that someone had stuffed a role of music down his instrument bell end. Well it was Christmas and whoever it was may have thought he was playing too loud!

Catherine Gilbert has reminded us of a story when `her Dad Eric Gilbert once got left behind by the bus at the Coronation Club in Armthorpe whilst doing 'collecting duties' at Christmas. Catherine says we picked him up later and she is sure that he was quite happy to have a break and few pints whilst waiting. (It must run in the family because you will hear later about Catherine getting left behind in a motor way Services)

It is surprising what happens in some of these once popular meeting places (public houses) and I say the words meeting places because several of the older band members when they were of the recognized age would often frequent pubs especially where we may have given a concert during the summer periods – Wheatley Hotel where we were always made welcome by Mr. Lancaster and the Benbow in Intake again where we were made very welcome by the landlady in this case, Mrs Saddington. The Benbow was located on Armthorpe Road (Intake) a couple of miles from Armthorpe. This was the main bus route from Doncaster to Armthorpe. Anyway, way by the time that John Middleton and myself reached the age of 18 or so and I could visit John at College in Newcastle (free, due to my relationship with British Rail whom I worked for) had started 'daring' the other to do something – challenge. Anyway, being in the summer and John being back home for the summer, we decided to go to the Benbow after the band practice for a pint. As the weather was nice we sat outside on the front grass and at the time the Benbow boasted 3 or 4 large beech trees. I bet you can't climb that tree John said, well having been brought up in Park Avenue where we had a very long garden which went down to the wood so climbing was for some – Me, second nature.

The dare was worth £1.00 so off I went and reached the top of the tree thereby winning the bet. Only to be chiselled by my mother a few days later! Why were you at the top a tree outside the Benbow? It was sometime before I did find out how she knew but apparently mother had a friend who was on a passing bus and saw me so the next time she saw my mother she said why was your Alan at the top of one of those trees in front of the Benbow!

Anyway, after one particularly adventurous Christmas Eve when some of the older members perhaps over indulged it was decided that we would restrain 'ourselves' a little and go back to somebody's house. This was always after midnight, and I remember when they came to my parents rather modest terraced Coal Board House, we had the front room bulging, people sat on the stairs and outside in the front garden. My mother and father loved it and often commented on it years and years later.

Well from this, eventually became another regular practice which has now become the customary visit to the Barber household on Christmas Eve, but not my parents but Barber Junior (me). On leaving the Band in the 80's after getting married, starting a family and progressing at work etc we always enjoyed their visit to our house, Gillian and myself on Christmas Eve. The band would come around 5.30 / 6.00 pm and at that time would play mainly for family and friends, but then has happens due only to inevitable age-related problems, numbers started to dwindle. Today however and for the past six or seven years, numbers have increased and as many as 40 plus enjoy a selection of carols by the band together with a drink, some nibbles, mince pies and sausage rolls. (We now have the great grandchildren of the parents of one of the founder members of the Band). How life moves on – 50 years and still going!

Before we leave Christmas carolling – a short explanation relating to a couple of the verses in the Anonymous Poem at the start of section 3. I remember the incident because it was close to one's heart, and happened racing down the Cul-de-Sac where Mr. & Mrs Prescott lived, parents of Steve and David. The road was icy and had not been gritted and it was 6.00 O'clock when the incident happened before we had ventured into the Pubs. (That's my interpretation of events and I am sticking to it).

The Band as well as featuring on the Radio in the 70's was also seen on television. Probably the first occasion was in the mid 70's around 1976/77) when for some reason we were asked to play on 'Its A Knockout'. I remember being in the middle of a big stadium in Huddersfield, but I am not sure of why or the reason behind it. I have been told recently that someone in the Studio said – 'Is this the only piece they know?' (It may have been Stuart Hall and that's why he is being entertained in her Majesty's prison!)

CHAPTER 19

THE BAND BECOMES INTERNATIONAL

Getting back to our Story we are by now about 16 years down the timeline -1980 and that was when the Band first became truly international in playing terms. (See reference to Amsterdam Trip 1972. I remember the date well because it nearly caused a divorce before the wedding ever taking place. One of the members of the Band (AB) proposed to another member of the Bass Section of the Band, a Miss Gillian Robinson, and the wedding it was decided would be on the 5th April 1980. This would allow us to have a few days holiday for a honey moon during the Easter break, because later in the year I had some exams to pass at College and was due to take part in a major canoeing expedition to the Himalayas. It was also the time the band was invited to Germany, to Braunshardt close to Darmstadt. The reason for the visit I am told started with another local band at Chesterfield who already had connections with Darmstadt. Alec Dinning the Band Master at Chesterfield was asked to visit Braunshardt because of the connections but did not want to go. Subsequently he got in touch with Eddie Mangham the band secretary and as usual Eddie jumped at the opportunity. (He was now becoming something of an expert getting AEB abroad having 'cut' his teeth with our trip to Amsterdam.)

What a great idea we said, we're up for that. Unfortunately, the visit was to take place the week before Easter, the week leading up to the 'said' Wedding when two of the Bass Players were about to get married. One half of the future matrimonial relationship was all for it, (and boy what a stag night you could have!) the second half however did not show as much enthusiasm. She just said, Alan, we are getting married!! The Band went to Germany and was back in time to provide a guard of honour with their instruments as the 'newlyweds' came out of church.

So, having narrowly avoided another world war here in Doncaster, the band did keep its promise and visited Germany. So, with envy I relate some of the stories from this first International exchange of Armthorpe Elmfield Band and of course their visit to Germany.

The relationship with Braunshardt actually started the previous year when Braunshardter Dorfschwalben Jugendorchester visited Armthorpe to play with the band. The visit happened in October from the 20th – 26th, 1979.

Here is a letter received from Mr. Volz the manager of the visiting band. (There have been several comments about 'Little Swallows' during conversations with some of the original band members, now the story is revealed!) Please note that it is not always easy to get a direct translation from German in to our language so please interpret it as you wish, and I am sure that you will get the 'gist' of what is meant.

Dear Mr. Griffiths, Mr. Mangham,

Many thanks for your invitation to be your guests. We are all very proud and happy to be here in Doncaster together with you.

First, I have to surrender many hearty greetings from our Singing Club 'Frohshinn" (translated perhaps in Happy to be) and its manager Mr. W Volz. And even so many thankful greetings from those German parents who have been left at home.

We, the 'Braunshardter Dorfschwalben (translated as 'Village Swallow') are the youngest members of the Frohsinn Club. Look at us, there are girls and boys from 10 years old up to 60 years (me)

Our little band is only 4 years old, and therefore, maybe in using their instruments they will not be so perfect here and there but nevertheless that is not the education aim for me. Being and feeling as a teacher

I want to spend happiness by our tunes, we play to young and old people, to poor and rich, to Germans and to English friends like today.

I want to attain the ribbon we are tying today that may become the beginning of a real friendship between Elmfield/ Armthorpe and Braunshardt/Weiterstadt, between England and Germany.

Here are some facts of where we come from,

Braunshardt is a little village of about 1600 inhabitants, and since 5 years coupled with Weiterstadt. Nowadays Weiterstadt has grown up to ca. 18000 inhabitants. There are 5 miles to Darmstadt, the County City and Darmstadt is the sister town to Chesterfield and is situated in midst of the Rhein – Main triangle, one of the busiest parts of Western Germany.

In Braunshardt there is an old castle where the famous Queen Louise of Prussia had spent her childhood 250 years ago. In Braunshardt there is a little elementary school, too and I am headmaster of it.

All my young musicians have been my pupils before, none of them had had an instrument and was not able to read any notes before. So 4 years ago I started with 4 trumpets, 3 accordions and 2 clarinets. Now I am happy to present you my band so as you can see them here. (This replicates the similar beginnings of Armthorpe Elmfield Band, but I cannot recall being called after a bird!)

So I do wish for you English Juveniles and for us German young musicians to spend these days together as an event, we'll never forget in our further life. To become real friends.

Well it was a truly memorable occasion with many concerts billed as International Concerts featuring Armthorpe Elmfield Band and from Germany Braunshardter Dorfschealben Jugendorchester – 'Braunshardt Little Swallows, entertaining Parents, Patrons and Friends, Staff at Elmfield House Youth Club, Members of Armthorpe Parish Council, The Mayor, and members of Doncaster Metropolitan Borough Council, and the local people of our area. As well as the concerts, visits took place to the City of York, including the Minster and the Railway Museum, Herringthorpe Valley Sports Centre for swimming, roller skating and table tennis, Robin Hood Country, Derbyshire, visit to 'Blue John Mine' and Chatsworth House, and a visit to Doncaster Mansion House.

Not bad for a first attempt Mr. Mangham!

The following is the parting letter to our first foreign visitors:

When you arrived for a week in Doncaster, we were happy, that we could welcome such friendly visitors, and as this week has gone on, a warm friendship has developed in spite of difficulties with the language.

I see the time had come and you must return to Germany. We wish you a safe and happy journey and hope that your trip holds good memories for you.

We will not say goodbye but Auf Wiederschen and we hope that it is not long until we can renew our friendship in Braunshardt.

So, the following Year Armthorpe visited Braunshardt. The second International expedition of the Armthorpe Elmfield Band.

Eddie Mangham being greeted by Mr. Volz at Braunshardt

Robert starts, and tells his story about that very first time in Germany visiting Darmstadt. Being a local lad an all that, especially being brought up on a pint a lager with double lime and not wine, it was of no surprise that he did not particularly like the offerings provided by their German hosts. So not wishing to appear ungrateful or impolite decided that he would pour his wine into the glass of his fellow Double 'B' player – Dennis Draycott who being a little older and maybe a bit more experienced in such things duly obliged. (Either that or he wasn't aware of what was happening). Anyway, all good things must come to end – some in more unfortunate ways, for example when Dennis fell off the stage!

This was the start, and several more visits have taken place to Germany, together with visits from our friends over there in Germany to Armthorpe, but now it is to Herten, Doncaster's Twin Town. There was however a gap from 1980 until around 1989/90.

The visits that now take place usually every fourth year is the result of Doncaster twinning with Herten in Germany and as you will hear later is still carried out.

The Spielmannszug Disteln-Bachum Band which our Band is associated with was formed in 1958 by three men. The three men were Mr. Drees, Mr. Kolecki and Mr. Hoppe. They joined up with the old shooting Guild of Disteln-Bachum and the first public appearance was an outdoor concert in 1959. By this time there were 20 musicians. In the next few years the group played at several competitions and at official concerts, and were always a welcome sight and sound. Sadly, in 1986, after a short illness, Mr. Drees passed away and Willi-Bernd, his son took over the position of musical director.

Willi-Bernd Drees was the third child of Wilhelm and Elizabeth Drees. Willi was born October 1948 in Herten-Disteln. From April 1st, 1955 to March 31st 1963 he attended the Catholic school in Herten-Disteln.

On April 1st, 1963 he began his apprenticeship at the coal mine. After a 3-year apprenticeship he carried on working as a coal miner until 31st January 1971. From 1971 until 1976 Willi-Bernd was hoping to have a successful career as a sportsman but unfortunately a serious illness meant that he could not carry on.

On 1st September 1978 as a result of the illness Willi-Bernd began to train as a clerk, and successfully completed the training in 1980. From then until his retirement on 31st October 2008 he worked as an administrative employee for miner's guild health insurance company in nearby Bochum. Now Will-Bernd is happy to enjoy his retirement and his music.

Haydn with Willi, and the mayor of Herten behind, at Armthorpe Community Centre.

The band under Willi-Bernd have made many public appearances with twin towns of Herten; Schneeberg in Saxony, Germany, Arras in France and of course Doncaster which the band is keen to keep up. At the time that the article was written in 2010 the band had 20 active members and five children learning.

So, following the little brief history of Spielmannszug Disteln-Bachum band we carry on with a few stories from the visits.

The first of these regular visits to Herten must have been memorable because I have been told about the pudding mix by many who went on the trip. So, when the band went to Germany on this next occasion, and this time with the support of a prominent Local Councillor, Tony Socket, who was always keen to strike up 'twinning' relationships

Spielmannszug Disteln-Bachum band

with foreign countries, and no doubt was instrumental in both the planning and arranging of the trip. The visit was to Herten and Arthur Lowcock relates his personal memories, 'it was the first time I had been abroad and on the bus, there was a gentle man that did wood craft, and also a chef from the Danum Hotel that took some Yorkshire pudding mixture on the bus with him. No doubt this was to provide the German hosts with a true Yorkshire delicacy! Anyway, when we arrived in Germany and went out the next day the mix' had spilt all over the bus which then had to be cleaned up before going out to find some more ingredients so that they could make the aforementioned delight.'

Catherine Watson also refers to this German visit and says, I remember one of the first German visits that we did was to Herten when Tony Socket came along. We were playing a street festival. My memories whilst a little vague I do recall a Chef who came to especially make "Yorkshire puddings" at this event and the pudding mixture was transported in bowls all the way on the coach. I am sure there was some disaster with this, which is what Arthur has alluded to.

Arthur continues his own story, 'We stopped in a youth hostel and I remember George King was with us and on the Saturday night when we arrived back to the hostel there was a bar, so we could have a drink. George King got talking to this man at the bar, then started singing to him, which was George all over (apparently). However, Arthur said we somehow found out the 'said' Gentleman was a rather 'friendly' character, (perhaps too friendly!) so there on after, George was christened 'Boy George' which he took in good fun'. I have heard that one of George's favorites whilst entertaining (unofficially) was performing the 'Stripper' so that's perhaps why the German Gentlemen was particularly interested in him !

Whilst this little story is about the bus, it was not concerning the band members but the driver and happened when the band visited Germany in 2004. Well with today's technology of Satellite Navigation Systems (Navis as they are called by Germans) and GPS positioning via mobiles and of course the Collins / AA Road map of Europe one wonders why it is still possible to get lost, but I am reliably informed that is what happened. The driver got slightly lost going around London on the way, just getting to the Eurotunnel in time. A very full weekend including many Parties and celebrations, and on the last day we were up at 5.00am to commemorate the new 'King'. We marched around the town in a parade with other bands, then straight back on to the bus for the return. We drove round Ghent twice on the way home and only just made the train again! We could have done with Robert on the way home, as the bus broke down, and had to be fixed using the light from a mobile phone!

Whilst I never actually participated in one of these visits to Germany, I have a story to tell about a person I met whilst working for a Company in South Africa. I had been asked to visit Johannesburg to get involved in some design work for Depot Improvements for the Passenger Rail Agency of South Africa. This was in 2013. I had been there a couple of weeks and was due to be flying back to the UK on this particular Saturday. We were staying in a private Lodge owned by the Company that I was working for. There were other people in the lodge, an acquaintance from Taiwan, a belgian guy and someone from Germany. We were carrying out different work for the railways but not on the same projects. Anyway, on my very last day I went to the veranda after I had finished my packing because the weather was quite nice - just getting over winter. A gentleman by the name of Klaus Kesser came and sat with me and we started chatting. When he heard that I was flying back to the UK he said where are you flying to? Manchester, I said. Oh, I have a friend near Manchester. I thought, here we go again, I have heard this many times before whilst working abroad, when someone finds out that you are from the UK they will often say, I have a friend in London, his / her name is XXX do you know him / her? So, I was expecting the same!!

However, what happened next came as a bit of a surprise, and will certainly be that of the reader I am sure, but it is perfectly true. Klaus asked if I lived in Manchester and I said no, I live about 65/70 miles away. Oh, where's that he said. Doncaster was the reply. Oh, I have a friend that lives near there, Fred and Barbara Paling, they live in a place called Armthorpe. I have another friend called Haydn Griffiths, he is the Conductor of Armthorpe Elmfield Band. I then had to tell him that in fact Fred lives less than 100m from where I live, whom I know well, and I also was a founder member of Armthorpe Brass Band, and that they still come to play at my house every Christmas Eve. I then had to go to the airport to catch my flight.

Klaus being presented with a Band photograph by Haydn

Having met Klaus several thousand miles away from Armthorpe in South Africa and then wondering what a coincidence, and for him to mention Fred and Barbara Paling I can now put the pieces together because of The Spielmannszug Disteln-Bachum Band, their relationship with the old shooting Guild of Disteln-Bachum and the fact that both Fred and Klaus had an interest in shooting and as consequence struck

up a close relationship. In fact, in 2004 the Band attended a shooting festival. Where the King is chosen by the very sensible method of everyone (including our Band Members!) shooting at a carved Eagle suspended from a tower. The person who finally brings down the Eagle is pronounced King for the next 5 Years! Far better than local elections.

The eagle all ready to be shot at!

The new King is congratulated by his shooting club colleagues, and 'crowned' by Klaus.

I have seen Klaus on a couple of occasions since and he still he tells stories of when he stayed with Barbara and Fred in his big white house. Klaus also reminds us here in Armthorpe of Yorkshire Day and sends out a flyer – Hip Hip Hooray to all friends of Armthorpe, with best regards, Klaus Kessen (Yorkshireman Honorary).

Klaus and his wife flying the flag after being woken early in the morning following the new Kings Coronation, by the Disteln-Bachum Spielmannszug Band, a bleary eyed Armthorpe Elmfield Band observed very bemused!

A newspaper article of June 11, 2010 sums up the relationship.

Musicians from Doncaster's twin town in Germany are continuing to maintain their links with the borough even though Mayor Peter Davies said he was against the idea of twinning.

Doncaster Central MP Rosie Winterton, and the Civic Mayor, Margaret Pinkney were among the guests who attended a combined concert at Armthorpe Community Centre which was put on by Armthorpe Elmfield Junior and Senior Band and Disteln-Bachum Spielmannszug Band.

The concert was held to celebrate many years of friendship between the bands from Doncaster and Herten, Germany, dating back to the 1980's. Afterwards Rosie said, 'This is a long-standing friendship between Herten and Doncaster which is now in its 21st year. It was a fantastic concert, very much enjoyed by everybody there'.

The final comment which has been brought to mind of which our German friends from Herten may be held in esteem with some of the members of the band is something to do with one of their players who played the cymbals having something to do with sie hat ein grossen ??? (not sure what that is but it may emanate from Bristol oder Bristols!

On a similar note but relating to extraordinary coincidences my work took me to Taiwan where I worked on the Taiwan High Speed rail Project. Any way as my work progressed I found I was spending more time away from Taipei and at the other end of the Island at a place called Koushung. On one occasion, I was there around 2006 and I'd arrange to meet a work colleague in a bar across the road from the Hotel. Well whilst it might rain a lot in Taiwan it is also usually very warm so here we were standing at the bar having a pint talking about work and what we had been doing when the barmaid came across and started caressing Adrian my colleagues arm as he has some tattoos. They like tattoos here he said. Then she said what's your name – he said Jones and then turned to me and said they can't say Adrian. Then turning to me she said what's your name, I replied Alan. She couldn't pronounce that, so I said Barber, so she said Bob. I said OK that will do.

Anyway, we decided to have something to eat so moved away from the Bar. I did notice another Westerner come in but paid little attention to him until he came across to us. 'Tha' calls you Bob dunt thee?' I said, 'no they call me Alan actually', to which he said 'she said you were called Bob'. I said 'it doesn't matter it's a long story'. Anyway, he says, 'where are you from?' 'UK' was my reply, yes but where? Yorkshire. Well the gentlemen swore. 'Where abouts in Yorkshire?' I told him Doncaster. He swore again, 'where abouts in Doncaster? – Armthorpe was my reply. He swore worse this time then he said,' do you know Bob Waldock?' I said yes through Scouting. (Bob came from Rossington and had come to Armthorpe to be foreman of the Blacksmiths Shop at the pit where Haydn worked.) The conversation immediately continued with, 'do you know Eric Hepworth' and I said 'Yes, I know him through scouting and canoeing'. He then said, 'do you know Haydn Griffiths?' and I said, 'yes, I do. I was a founder member of the Band, and all three come to my house on Christmas Eve.'

So here we were 8,000 miles away from Doncaster and I bump into Bob Ferguson who used to work as an electrician at the colliery and worked in the same shop as these three.

So, there we are, The World gets smaller!

Parlez vous Francaise and what's that hole in the floor for?

The next story following on with the Continental theme relates to when the Band went to France. Catherine recollects:'

I think I was 13 so it was around 1985, and we stayed in a gymnasium on makeshift beds. I have a few funny memories of this trip, please note here that this was an Educational Trip and yes Mr. Socket did have an involvement!

The "men folk" were playing football with a basketball whilst in their undies, shoes and socks, (as you do?) and it was getting very competitive. Glynn ended up with a damaged hand and had to have his wedding ring cut off because of the swelling, and knew he would be in the bad books when he got back home!

I will never forget seeing Mr. G in his Y fronts going off to the loo early in the morning – I am scarred for life.

I wonder if this was part of Tony Sockets organizational skills as he was Head of Doncaster Youth Service at the time!

As we all know our French 'friends' have some different ways of going to the ablutions, and coming from Armthorpe you don't get many holes in the floor, so I guess it was no surprise when Dennis was standing over a hole in the floor (which was the toilet) thinking it was a shower and wondering where the water was going to come from!

At the festival Catherine went to the loo with Roz and got locked in the toilet with no way out, and no way of communicating with a load of French people. Since then she says that I never lock a toilet door if it's sides and door fall to the floor and rise to the ceiling (i.e. no other way out)!!

On the way home, the bus stopped at a service station for a PNB and Catherine was the last out of the ladies, she trotted over to the bus which seemed to be further away than she remembered, only to discover that they had set off without her, (it must run in the family see comment about Dad getting left in the Club on Christmas Eve!). Fortunately, someone realised she was missing moments before getting back on the motorway!

On a final note, I have just been made aware why this trip had such a significant effect on Catherine, it might be something to do with falling in love with a French Lad!!

(I am advised by another member that this love story relates to the said Miss Gilbert and the mayor's son. Apparently, a jumper had been left behind and the son came on the bus and handed it over. On leaving he said – Je t'aime. I'm not sure if I understand all this but does it mean I Love you?)

Still in France, apparently the Band was on stage during a Rock Concert and were expected to play during dinner, between courses and it was a five-course meal, and I am told there was excessive amounts of that liquid which is often consumed by the French at meal times. Possibly a first for a brass band in support of a rock concert, and of course we here in the UK have not been accustomed to five course dinners since the Middle Ages.

CHAPTER 20

WHO CAN WALK ON WATER?

Leaving the International Travels these next few stories relate closer to home – Cleethorpes by the Sea which is not really on the Sea but the River Humber where you had to have a 3d ride on a tractor to get to the water because you couldn't see it when the tide went out

Catherine can't remember the year exactly, but it must have been mid 1980's around 1984 when we were invited to play in an entertainment contest that took place in Cleethorpes. Us "young ones" would play in the contest at the Winter Gardens, then nip over to the sports centre for a swim. We also used to do the same (go for a swim) in between playing at Peasholme Park in Scarborough. (This must be where she got her liking for water from see below!)

Regarding the entertainment contest, I seem to remember that we were invited to play in the Humberside band of the year 1985/86 because they didn't have enough bands from the area, and we ended up winning! Obviously at that age we were more interested in the 'Social' side of the band!!

Another Seaside story was when we played in Peasholme Park, Scarborough, Mr. G decide to play a particular tune that we tended to play leading into the interval where we all went off in turn whilst doing a few bars conducting. Playing Jamie's Patrol as it was called, often brought intrigued looks from the audience because obviously they did not know what was happening, but on this occasion, it was even more interesting because as Catherine said, we were playing on an Island next to the water, and the only place to walk off was around the edge of the band stand which was about 1 foot wide. Catherine tripped over a wire and was due to take an 'early' bath and only narrowly avoided falling into the lake, when someone caught her. Mind you she would have easily been seen due to the red hair! (Maybe someone might have 'fished' her out thinking she was a fisherman's float!) See reference below to change of hair colour at Epworth!

I also heard a similar story when playing in Peasholme Park and that they had to get over to the island by boat, which was OK but those with smaller bladders had to cross their legs until they were boated off. What a relief!!

Again, she recalls another funny story which is personal to her, but as she says always makes her smile.

I used to have long blonde curly hair, then I had it all cut off really short, and dyed it red!!. We played at Epworth Church on two occasions but a year apart and afterwards when I had played a solo on the flugelhorn, this old man came up to her and complimented her on the performance. He then proceeded to tell her about the previous flugelhorn horn player who was "really good" but she had long blond hair. Catherine said, yes that was me, but he said no, she had long curly hair, and She said I was like that, it was me, I just had my hair cut, but he wouldn't believe it was me!

Whilst we are on with Solos and we have heard about the wonderful solos that were played at the concerts in Epworth I am reminded of another occasion when a trombone soloist did not 'rise' to the occasion!

Shall we just say that once upon a time the band had a member called Andy and what a fine trombone he had, he would play every note he could see, see every note he could play, and if he didn't see a note he wouldn't play it. Well as said unfortunately there was an occasion when what happened didn't go according to plan, or more precise to the agenda on the programme because according to it there should have been a bass trombone solo. Can you imagine the band playing and then waiting for the soloist who had fallen asleep? Can you Adam and Eve it?

Another couple of well known sayings from the man himself, "Gentlemen scrape your instrument with sound, and play like you have never played before - together!"

As I have said before, the band has had to share the stage with many different people and celebrities etc. in the past, and on one occasion a bird! This was not one of those members of the opposite sex to a male which is often referred to as a 'Bird' where we come from, it was a member of a 'Birds of Prey' display team at a concert gala where the band were playing.

Anyway, as the story goes the "Chief Falcon" was called upon to carry out its 'Piece de Resistance' and perform some magical flying stunts, which sounded to me as though, perhaps it didn't quite go according to plan! The Band in the meantime had just finished playing Silver Hill a hymn that they had been playing since God was a Lad, but on this occasion had they got it wrong? Because no sooner had the 'Performances' taken place an announcement was made, or more precisely it was heard over the loud speaker system, 'well that's a load of rubbish, dreadful, absolutely dreadful. (It was noticed however that the bird got stuffed back into a box – whoops!!)

In 2012 the band was fortunate to make the National Finals which were held in Cheltenham. This said contest was the back end of the year and followed another yet successful visit to Germany. And guess what? What do you think Germany is good at other than making cars, beer of course! So, armed with some duty free German beer the bus sets off for Cheltenham. First part of the mission accomplished.

However, on the way to rehearsal the bus breaks down (where have we heard this before?) unfortunately on this occasion we did not have Mr. 'fixit' Bob on board and another bus had to come and recover the situation. Everything off – instruments, beer the lot!

Well another bus did come to take them to the Race Course, but this was a smaller bus and to cap it all, the driver declared that he wouldn't be stopping so they had to take everything off and carry it in. So here they were still trying to get into the event with instruments and smuggled beer, and of course what do you say to security about a crate of German Pilsner?

One might say the sun shines on the righteous because as luck would have it, the security guard that met them just happened to be Jonathon Tingy and an ex-member of the band and I think he was so pleased to see Griff and some of the old faces that he totally missed the beer. (Or did he just turn a 'blind' eye, anyway it was a good job they succumbed to a little smuggling because when they eventually arrived at their hotel there was no food and the bar was closed!

And finally, do you know why you can't play one handed, because you can't play with two. (I am told that these little sayings became so interesting that one of the bands top cornet players actually did work for an A level on sayings of the Old Man!

CHAPTER 21

TO CONCLUDE

As we bring this story to a conclusion it is not really the end because the Band continues – still playing lots of engagements taking part in competitions and contests and of course marching.

We could continue, and I am positively sure that if we were to continue with our little get togethers – reminiscing, do you recall the time when? Can you remember when, and so on and so on, however to enable the band as it is today with existing members and still a few of the originals to get the credit they are due, it has been decided to draw it to a conclusion.

When Richard Stengal wrote of Nelson Mandela – Portrait of an Extraordinary Man he spent nearly 3 years collaborating with him on his autobiography and traveling with him everywhere, becoming a cherished friend and colleague. Unfortunately we don't have that long so in only a third of the time we have tried to accumulate the happenings of half a Century – yes portraying an extraordinary person with a passion for banding who has spent a 'life time' encouraging, cajoling, nurturing but above all helping people young and old – particularly young people to pursue a path that perhaps they would not have considered, and as said in different parts of this book, brought credit to themselves, the Band and Armthorpe / Doncaster the area from which they came from.

I started off to write about 'Inspiration' and as I gaze back in time one can only wonder about the Inspiration that Haydn Griffiths has given to people, Band Members, Supporters and followers of the Band, parents of Band Members, Organisations, Institutions and of course Personal Individuals. Whilst it would be difficult to try and elaborate on this, I am sure that as 'We' progressed through the book, one will appreciate the Inspiration that emanates from the 'Man' in the middle.

It has been said in the song: -

We've had our ups and we've had our downs,

We've had our days and not done bad,

Just think of the Trophies and Medals we've had.

But we are still here, through thick and thin, forever tackling 'hardships', and adversities but celebrating the 'Good Times' with one main objective to please the Man' in the middle.

When we are in the Band room there's only one in charge,

There's no need to say who that is, he's rather bald and large.

Haydn Griffiths OBE – Musical Director of Armthorpe Elmfield Band.

This covers the Period from 1964 – 2015.

BAND PICTURES

Armthorpe Elmfield Band 2002

Armthorpe Elmfield Band at The Dell, Hexthorpe, Doncaster. 2003

A photograph from 1953, showing Markham Mail Colliery Band at The Dell in Hexthorpe. This was published in The Doncaster Advertiser in October 1995. Haydn Griffiths Top Right.

Armthorpe Elmfield Band 2014

APPENDIX I

1 – CONTEST /COMPETITION RESULTS

Also previously known as: Armthorpe High School Band

| http://brassbandr | http://brassbandr | | **Section:** | **Fourth / Third** |

Region: Yorkshire
Wins: **12**
Second Places: **15**
Third Places: 10

Date	Contest	Test Piece	Section	Points	Position
1970					
1971					
1972	CISWO Regional Competition Sheffield	Garland of Classics – William Rimmer	4th	182	7th
1973	CISWO Regional Competition Sheffield	Music For the Royal Fireworks– Handel		188	1st
1973	Worksop Music Festival	Salzburg Suite – Dennis Wright		90	
1973	Pontefract Music Festival	Music for the Royal Fireworks		90	
1973	Festival Hall National Association Boys Clubs	Music for the Royal Fireworks			
1973	CISWO National Contest Blackpool	The Ancient Temple – Eric Ball	4th	182	4th
1974	National Brass Band Championship, Yorkshire Regional Qualifying - Bradford	Four Little Maids – John Carr	4th	176	3rd
1974	Pontefract Music Festival	Four Little Maids – John Carr		93	
1974	National Brass Band Finals – Hammersmith Town Hall. London	Youth Salutes A Master – Eric Ball	4th	176	12th
1975	CISWO Regional Competition Sheffield	The Ancient Temple – Eric Ball	4th	192	1st
1975	CISWO National Contest Blackpool	Festival Suite – Johnson		190	1st
1976	CISWO Regional Competition Sheffield	Promenade -		183	2nd
1976	CISWO National Contest Blackpool				
1977	CISWO Regional Competition Sheffield			174	
1977	Doncaster Entertainment Contest				

Date	Contest	Test Piece	Section	Points	Position
1977	City of Leicester Brass Band Festival			179	
1978	Doncaster Entertainment Competition – Semi Final			163	
1978	National Brass Band Yorkshire Regional Qualifying - Bradford	Mexican Fiesta	4th	175	5th
1978	CISWO Regional Competition Sheffield	Mexican Fiesta	4th	187	2nd
1978	Britvic National Contest Blackpool	The princess and the Poet – Eric Ball	4th	187	3rd
1978	Doncaster Entertainment Competition			167	
1979	Doncaster Entertainment Competition Semi Final			176	
1979	CISWO Regional Competition Sheffield	The Winters Tale	4th	185	3rd
1979	City of Leicester Brass Band Festival				
1980	CISWO Regional Competition			185	
1980	Yorkshire Regional Qualifying - Bradford			187	
1980	Britvic National Contest Blackpool			194	
1981	Yorkshire Regional Qualifying - Bradford				
1981	CISWO Regional Competition Sheffield			182	
1981	Britvic National Contest Blackpool			180	
1982	CISWO Regional Competition Sheffield			180	

Date	Contest	Test Piece	Section	Points	Position
1982	Yorkshire Regional Qualifying - Bradford			185	
1982	Yorkshire & Humberside BBA Contest			185	
1982	Joshua Tetley Leeds Open				
1982	Harrogate and District BBA Contest			178	
1983	Yorkshire Regional Qualifying - Bradford				
1983	CISWO Regional Competition Sheffield			187	
1983	Yorkshire & Humberside BBA Contest			179	
1983	Britvic National Contest Blackpool				
1984	Yorkshire Regional Qualifying - Bradford				
1984	CISWO Regional Competition Sheffield			184	
1984	Yorkshire & Humberside BBA Contest				
1984	Joshua Tetley Leeds Open			185	
1985	CISWO Regional Competition Sheffield			174	
1985	Yorkshire Regional Qualifying - Bradford			184	
1985	Yorkshire & Humberside BBA Contest			173	
1985	Joshua Tetley Leeds Open			189	
1985	National Championship of Great Britain				

Date	Contest	Test Piece	Section	Points	Position
1986	Yorkshire Regional Qualifying - Bradford			172	
1986	CISWO Regional Competition Sheffield				
1986	Yorkshire & Humberside BBA Contest			179	
1986	Joshua Tetley Leeds Open			176	
1986	Britvic National Contest Blackpool				
1987	CISWO Regional Competition Sheffield				
1987	Yorkshire Regional Qualifying - Bradford			171	
1987	Joshua Tetley Leeds Open				
1988	CISWO Regional Competition Sheffield			181	
1988	Yorkshire Regional Qualifying - Bradford			181	
1988	Pontins Southport Contest			174	
1988	Thorne Entertainment Contest			168	3rd
1988	Britvic National Contest Blackpool			182	
1989	Yorkshire Regional Qualifying - Bradford			185	
1989	CISWO Regional Competition Sheffield			178	
1989	National Championship of Great Britain				
1989	National Mineworkers CISWO			187	
1990	CISWO Regional Competition Sheffield			185	

Date	Contest	Test Piece	Section	Points	Position
1990	National Championship of Great Britain				
1990	Pontins Hemsby Contest				
1990	National Mineworkers CISWO			185	
1991	Yorkshire Regional Qualifying - Bradford			179	
1991	CISWO Regional Competition Sheffield			170	
1991	National Mineworkers CISWO				
1992	Yorkshire Regional Qualifying - Bradford				
1992	National Mineworkers CISWO			180	
1992	Pontins Southport Contest				
1993	Yorkshire Regional Qualifying - Bradford			176	
1993	National Mineworkers CISWO			186	
1993	National Mineworkers CISWO			185	
1994	CISWO Regional Competition Sheffield			181	
1994	Yorkshire Regional Qualifying - Bradford			186	
1994	National Championship of Great Britain			78	
1994	National Mineworkers CISWO				
1995	Yorkshire Regional Qualifying - Bradford	Roco Variations	2nd	173	12

Date	Contest	Test Piece	Section	Points	Position
1996	Yorkshire Regional Qualifying - Bradford			179	
1996	National Mineworkers CISWO			186	
1997	Yorkshire Regional Qualifying - Bradford			171	
1997	National Mineworkers CISWO			171	
1998	Yorkshire Regional Qualifying - Bradford	Three Saints	3rd	183	8th
1998	National Mineworkers CISWO			184	
1999	Yorkshire Regional Qualifying - Bradford	Main Street	3rd	167	13th
2000	Yorkshire Regional Qualifying - Bradford	Narnia Suite		183	3
2000	National Mineworkers CISWO			180	
2001	Yorkshire Regional Qualifying - Bradford	Sinfonietta	3rd	188	1st
2001	National Mineworkers CISWO			178	
2001	National Mineworkers CISWO Blackpool		3rd	178	4th
2002	Yorkshire Regional Qualifying - Bradford	St. Austell Suite	3rd	177	5th
2002	National Mineworkers CISWO			188	

Date	Contest	Test Piece	Section	Points	Position
2003	Yorkshire Regional Qualifying - Bradford	Celestial Propect	2nd	167	11th
2003	Butlins Mineworkers Contest			175	
2004	Yorkshire Regional Qualifying - Bradford	Kaleidoscope	2nd	178	10th
2005	Yorkshire Regional Qualifying - Bradford	Tam O'Shanters Ride	3rd	176	6th
2006	Yorkshire Regional Qualifying - Bradford	Entertainments	3rd	173	9th
2007	Yorkshire Regional Qualifying - Bradford	Prelude and Jubilate	3rd	172	10th
2008	Yorkshire Regional Qualifying - Bradford	Four Cities Symphony	4th	173	4th
2009	Yorkshire Regional Qualifying - Bradford	The Talisman for Brass Band	4th		5th
2010	Yorkshire Regional Qualifying - Bradford	Labour and Love	3rd		12th
2011	Yorkshire Regional Qualifying - Bradford	Prelude, Song and Dance	4th		6th
2012	Yorkshire Regional Qualifying - Bradford	English Folk Song	4th		2nd
2012	National Championship of Great Brtitain	A British Isles Suite			9th

Date	Contest	Test Piece	Section	Points	Position
2013	Yorkshire Regional Qualifying - Bradford	Devon Fantasy	4th		6th
2014	Yorkshire Regional Qualifying - Bradford	Partita for Band	3rd		6th
2015	Yorkshire Regional Qualifying - Bradford	Five States of hange	3rd		9th
2016					

2 – CONSTITUTION AND RULES OF THE ARMTHORPE ELMFIELD BAND SUPPORTERS ASSOCIATION

1.   Name

The Association shall be called and known by the name of ARMTHORPE ELMFIELD BAND SUPPORTERS ASSOCIATION (herein after called "the Association".

2.   Objects

The objects of the Association shall be to promote the brass band movement with particular emphasis on the training and teaching and loan of instruments, uniforms, music and other necessary items for members of the Armthorpe Elmfield Band.

3.   Property

- The ownership of the whole of the musical instruments, music, uniforms and all property belonging to the Association shall be vested in Trustees who shall be the Chairman, of the Association, Fredrick Arthur Paling of the White House Armthorpe and Graham Shephard of 4 Church View, Campsall.

- The musical instruments, music, uniforms and all property belonging to the Association shall be insured in the name of the Association with a reputable insurance company by the Management Committee as hereinafter mentioned and such insurance should afford an indemnity against loss, fire theft or serious damage.

- The property of the Association shall not be sold or otherwise disposed of except with the consent of the trustees acting only in pursuance of the authority of the General Meeting hereinafter referred to. If any of the property belonging to the Association be disposed of or sold, the proceeds shall be for the purposes of the Association.

- If the Association be broken up or disbanded, the property belonging to the Association shall be sold or otherwise disposed of in such a manner as may be directed by the General Meeting and a resolution of such General meeting be passed with the support of at least seventy percent of the then membership (as distinct from members voting on such a resolution) shall be sufficient authority and instruction for the trustees to give their consent pursuant to clause 3 (c)

4 Membership

Membership of the Association shall be open to persons interested in the objects of the Association and who pay the association a minimum subscription rate which, subject to Clause 5 hereof, shall be £1.00 per annum, provided always that one membership subscription shall be deemed to cover membership of husband or wife or vice versa.

The person listed in the appendix A shall form the initial membership of the association.

5 Meetings

The membership shall meet in General Meeting at least once a year and the first meeting in each year shall be the Annual Meeting at which the following business shall be transacted.

- Appointment of Officers
- To receive a statement of the Audited accounts of the previous year.
- Report on the property of the Association.
- Election of Management Committee from the membership of the Association.

- Approval of a budget for the ensuing year.

- To decide the subscription rates for the ensuing year.

- Appointment of an Auditor to audit the accounts of the Association.

    The quorum shall be one third of the membership. The year shall commence of the first day of October.

6   Officers

The Officers of the Association shall be the Chairman, the secretary, the treasurer who shall be elected from the membership provided always that no member shall be appointed to any office unless such member has attained the age of 18 years.

7   Duties of the Officer

The duties of the secretary shall include, inter-alia, responsibility for calling all meetings, maintaining a record of all such meetings and a record of Association property. The secretary shall give not less than seven days prior notice of the date, venue and time for all meetings held either of the membership or management Committee hereinafter referred to.

The duties of the treasurer shall include, inter-alia, responsibility for the demand and collection of all moneys due to the Association, the safe keeping of all moneys of the Association, maintenance of insurance and proper records, presentation of a balance sheet annually and payment of accounts. He/She shall produce all such information as shall be required by the Auditors.

8   Management Committee

The Management Committee (hereinafter called the Committee") shall comprise of at least seven members additional to the Officers plus, ex-officio, the representative of the Director of Recreation and Services of the Doncaster Borough Council and the Musical Director of the Armthorpe Elmfield Band. The Committee shall have the day to day responsibility for the management of the Association and the authority to incur expenditure, a resolution of the Committee shall be the sole and sufficient authority for payments to be made to the treasurer.

Applications for membership shall be dealt with by the Committee except that any person whose application for membership is refused by the Committee may re-apply direct to the secretary for membership and the application shall be determined at the next General Meeting.

The Committee shall appoint from their membership persons to act as Chairman and Vice Chairman of the Committee respectively. The Committee shall meet not less than three times a year in accordance with arrangements to be made by the Committee and the quorum shall be three members. The Committee shall have a general power to co-opt to its membership additional members of the Association.

9   Band Accounts and Cheques

The Association shall operate a current account with Barclays Bank Limited.

The account shall be operated by the Treasurer and all cheques shall be signed by him/her and the Musical Director of the Armthorpe Elmfield Band or a nominated signatory from the management committee.

10   Patrons

The Committee may appoint as Patrons any member of the Association above the age of 18 years or any other interested person provided that such patrons shall pay a subscription of not less than the £1.00 per annum, or such other sum fixed by the General Meeting.

11   Loan of Property

The Committee shall authorize the loan of the property of the Association to the Armthorpe Elmfield Band on Such conditions as they shall deem necessary so as to control the use thereof and the arrangements for the inspection and return thereof. Provided always that it shall be a specific condition of loan of the property of the Association that no borrower shall use the said property to play other than for the Armthorpe Elmfield Band except with the prior consent of the Committee or the Musical Director.

12   Expulsion

The Committee may expel any member for misconduct, for non-attendance, for non-payment of subscription.

13   Interpretation

In the event of any question, matter or difference arising which is not covered by these rules, it shall be left to the Committee to decide, and their decision shall be binding as though a rule existed to meet the case.

14   Income

All monies received shall forthwith be paid into the bank account. Such monies shall only be used for the purpose of defraying the property costs, charges and expenses of and incidental to the administration and management of the Association, and of maintaining, repairing and, if and when the Trustees think fit, replacing the property of the Association.

15   Alterations

The rules may from time to time be altered or rescinded by a simple majority of those present and voting at any Special or Annual Meeting of the members of the Association, provided that notice in writing of the motion so as to amend or vary or rescind the rules shall have been sent to the secretary not less than one Calendar month before the date of such meeting.